Getting Through to People

Getting Through to People

Jesse S. Nirenberg, Ph.D.

Englewood Cliffs, N.J.
PRENTICE-HALL, INC.

28 27 26 25 24 23 22 PBK
10 9 8 7 6 5   RWD CLASSICS PBK

L. C. CATALOG CARD NO.: 63-15341

ISBN 0-13-354837-6 PBK

ISBN 0-13-355041-9 RWD CLASSIC PBK

PRINTED IN THE UNITED STATES OF AMERICA
35486-B&P

To Edna, Elizabeth, Sheila, and Nina

Contents

CONTENTS

Getting Through to People

1

The Problem of Getting
Through to People

Through words we try to touch each other's minds. And yet, although words flow freely, it is curious how seldom and how fleetingly minds meet. What keeps us from getting through to each other? How can we pierce the barrier?

The problem stems from two sources: one is being human; and the other is forgetting that others are human, too. If we talked to a robot, there would be no difficulty in getting through. The robot would accept our ideas without question and put them into action. The robot has no pre-existing attitudes which might conflict with our ideas; no emotion to distract him; no secrets to be kept; and no ego to be fed.

Unlike machines, we have an active inner life. In our inner world, emotions press for expression; wishes conflict with each other; unconscious, and often false, conceptions of the world suggest courses of action and attitudes which are unrealistic, but which we think are rationally based. In this inner world there are problems to be solved. One part of us continually tugs at the intellect to solve these unconscious problems, while another part of us pulls the intellect in another direction, toward working out the realistic problems of everyday life.

These unconscious problems vary from person to person. Some examples might be: How do I make everybody approve of me? How can I become a good person? How can I keep from getting hurt, falling ill, or dying? How can I get all the pleasure I want? How can I get more power? The intellect is prodded by these pleas while trying to attend to such realistic matters as getting to work, doing the job, getting along with one's mate, making and keeping friends, and rearing one's children.

For example, in trying to discuss problems rationally, people often find their conversations becoming cluttered by self-glorifying references, indirect bids for reassurance, and hostile allusions. Unconscious needs are pulling them away from logical thinking and talking and may obscure the original purpose of the conversation.

Is it any wonder that straight thinking, clear communication, and a meeting of minds are not easily achieved?

Five Human Characteristics That Work Against A Meeting Of Minds

Let's take a look at some human tendencies and how they interfere with a meeting of minds.

1. RESISTANCE TO CHANGE. We are all caught in a web of habit. But this web is quite comfortable and we are reluctant to give it up. The web feels safe, for we are both the spider and the fly.

Habit influences every thought, feeling, and action. While it governs such everyday things as the way we comb our hair, the way we like our eggs, which newspaper we read, and how neatly we dress, it also influences a tendency we might have to always ask somebody's advice before making a decision; or to get very annoyed over little things that get in our way; or to worry too much; or to feel that people are selfish and can't be trusted; or to think that we have to win every time.

Psychologists have found that just repeating an act doesn't make it a habit. In addition to repeating it there must be some gain in doing it. We cling to certain ways of thinking, feeling, and acting, not because we have always done it that way but because it serves some purpose for us. For example, if we have little confidence in our own judgment, we may always ask someone's advice before acting because it makes us feel more secure. We may feel that people are selfish because we want more from them than we have a right to expect. When we don't get it we call them selfish because the unpleasant alternative is to face the fact that we are selfish in our demands.

Habits are often very difficult to give up because the benefits we think we gain are too important to us. The gain may be real or imaginary; but as long as we feel we gain, we cling to the habit. And the more we seem to gain the stronger is the habit.

Let's listen in for a moment on a conversation between a company department head and a supervisor who works under him. Here we can see the supervisor's attitude toward his subordinates operating as a fixed habit and blocking communication between himself and his boss.

> DEPARTMENT HEAD: Tom, you've been doing a good job of supervising your unit but there's something I'd like to talk to you about. Some of your men have been complaining that you're always hopping on them whenever they make a mistake. But you never give them any credit for what they accomplish. You know a guy likes a pat on the back once in a while.
>
> SUPERVISOR: Why don't those guys grow up? What they want is a wet nurse. Well, I'm not going to baby them. I don't believe in coddling men.

> DEPARTMENT HEAD: Nobody's asking you to coddle them. But a man likes to be told how well he is doing. It's good for his morale and motivates him.
>
> SUPERVISOR: When a man's good he knows it. He doesn't need to be told. Give these fellows a good word and the next thing you know they'll ask for more money.
>
> DEPARTMENT HEAD: How about that fellow, Bob Grant? I understand he's doing fine, learning his job quickly and getting along well with the others. Do you ever give him a word of appreciation?
>
> SUPERVISOR: Bob's all right. But I'm not going to let him know about it; at least not yet. If I do, he'll become too satisfied with himself and start slackening off. I know these guys. You've got to keep them guessing, make them feel they're not doing well enough.

This supervisor is difficult to reach. He has a fixed attitude of distrust towards people. He is afraid that if he gives them any opportunity they will take advantage of him. He doesn't consider each individual on his merits but has already made up his mind before he even meets a person. One can't know why he feels this way without knowing him much better; but one possible explanation is that he feels that he, himself, can't be trusted and therefore expects that other people would do the same thing as he would do in any given situation. Therefore, it's safer not to trust. Let's take a look at some other barriers to communication.

2. THE URGE TO THINK ONE'S OWN THOUGHTS RATHER THAN LISTEN. Whenever you talk to another person you are competing for his attention. Your listener isn't wholly yours. His attention vacillates between what you are saying and what he is concerned about.

In order to hold his attention your talk has to matter more to him than anything else on his mind, whether it be his wife's visit to the doctor that morning, his children not doing so well in school, his own golf game, his boss's subtle hint that your listener might be in line for a step up soon, or the traffic ticket he shouldn't have gotten the night before because the stop sign he passed was covered with dirt and practically illegible.

Your listener's attention is fickle. It is drawn to anything that promises pleasure, excitement, or the solution of a problem. It scampers away from knotty problems and complex concepts. It is fragile and falls apart when stimulated by sudden sounds.

Often, when the individual is faced with difficult decisions that require a careful thinking through, attention drifts away into irrelevant by-paths; and it is pulled back only by the continual exercise of self-discipline. Even with that, attention drifts in and out of focus on a particular subject and the individual has little control over this.

You might try a little experiment for yourself. Pick any object in the room, for example, a lamp or a chair. Try concentrating on it, excluding all other thoughts. You will find that you cannot keep this up longer than about 5 or 10 seconds. Suddenly, you will find your field of attention filled with other images, and the lamp or chair will no longer be there. You bring it back to the lamp only to have it wander away in another few seconds.

If people's attention drifts in and out like this, how is it that they are able to comprehend each other in conversation? If they miss words, how can they understand the total thoughts being conveyed? The answer is that language provides sufficient redundancy and repetition so that we do not need to hear everything. The words we do hear carry enough of the meaning to communicate the essential thought.

For this reason, deliberate repetition is often useful in conversation. It helps an individual to avoid losing his listener. To make the repetition interesting, put it in different words.

However, when complex ideas are tightly packed into few words rather than being enlarged upon, contact tends to be lost. When each word is depended on to carry so much meaning, missing a few words can break contact completely. The listener loses the speaker and cannot find him again because the missing words are the key to the meaning of what follows.

Three Signs of Wandering Attention

You can detect wandering attention in your listener by three signs.

(a) ASKING UNNECESSARY QUESTIONS. One indication is his asking of questions whose answers were contained in what you have just talked about. If he had grasped what you said his questions would have been unnecessary.

Grasping what you said means more than just hearing it. He might hear it to the extent that he could repeat it back. But he could do this without really thinking about it to the extent of placing it in a total picture in relationship to other facts. Grasping ideas, that is, listening meaningfully, requires more than just hearing the words. It calls for fitting the ideas that are being heard into a total picture.

Meaningful listening is somewhat like putting together a jigsaw puzzle. Hearing the words is like receiving the pieces. But listening meaningfully is putting the pieces together to form a picture. When the listener asks questions that should have been unnecessary he has just been receiving the pieces but not putting them together.

(b) MAKING IRRELEVANT COMMENTS. Another indication of wandering attention is the making of irrelevant comments by the listener. Here the listener is not using the jigsaw pieces provided by the speaker to build the picture that the speaker has in mind. The listener is supplying his own pieces from a separate picture in his own mind.

These irrelevant comments indicate that the listener is strongly motivated not only to think about something else but also to talk about what he has in mind. This is more important to him than capturing the picture that the speaker is trying to communicate. The listener may need to show how clever he is by bringing in impressive ideas. And this need may be greater than his need to grasp what the speaker is saying. Or he may wish to improve on the conception that the speaker is presenting, and can't wait to do this in an orderly manner. He must take over direction of forming the concept.

It is also possible that the listener has emotions which are pressing for release, and he can't bear to wait until the speaker has developed the whole idea–picture. Instead, the listener intersperses irrelevant comments that represent discharges of anger, anxiety, guilt, or joy. For example, he may suddenly start talking about something that worries him; or may express irritation through a sarcastic remark.

(c) BRINGING UP AN ARGUMENT THAT HAS ALREADY BEEN ANSWERED. Another indication of wandering attention, somewhat related to the asking of unnecessary questions, is the repeating of an objection or argument by the listener when this objection or argument has already been answered. The answer never registered on the listener and as a result he was never moved from his original position. He is back where he started, as though the speaker had never spoken, and brings up again the same arguments as before.

For an example of two people talking to each other with neither focusing on the other's ideas, consider John and his wife, Mary, discussing vacation plans:

> JOHN: Say, Mary, we finally got the vacation schedules worked out. Mine's the last two weeks in July. That's not far off. We'd better make plans. I was thinking about that cottage on the lake we saw last summer.
>
> MARY: The last two weeks in July? That's wonderful! The hottest part of the summer. I'll have to buy some summer clothes. I don't think anything I've got fits me.
>
> JOHN: That cottage was very reasonable—$800. And a lake full of fish. I hope we can still get it. I think the kids'll be crazy about it, too.
>
> MARY: Do you know how much weight I put on since last summer? Eight pounds. I've got to start taking it off right now or I won't set foot on that beach. Remember how much fun we had at the shore last summer, John? The kids were crazy about it. You know, Tommy really learned to swim there—waves and all. I hope we can still get those same rooms.

As you can see, this discussion isn't really leading anywhere. John and Mary are both talking but they are not listening tc each other. They are tuned in only on their own inner pre-occupations. Each is forming his own pictures but not convey-ing them to the other person.

3. WISHFUL HEARING. Wishes have almost magical power. Sometimes they seem to hypnotize. Although we can't always have what we want when we want it, we often continue to wish for it; and sometimes this wish is so strong that it distorts our perceptions. We see and hear a world of our own making; and given a few isolated facts we jump to conclusions as though we couldn't bear to have some loose facts on our hands.

Any lawyer can tell you about the unreliability of witnesses. How a figure glimpsed for a moment on a dark night at an incredible distance will be positively identified in sworn testi-mony. He will also tell you about two witnesses completely disagreeing about the appearance of an individual seen at close range in bright daylight. Heard through walls or at a distance, a high-pitched sound is a shriek to some and laughter to others; and crying to one ear is singing to another. One person tells about a pleasant chat he overheard, which becomes a violent argument in the description of another observer.

Wishes color our lives, both brightly and darkly. We feel sure we are right even though we don't have much evidence. We are secretly convinced that we are more deserving of some reward than is our competitor. We are certain that someone whose tastes are different from ours has bad taste. We also wish harm to those we hate, and know that our own intentions are always the best.

While there are wishes for beauty, love, wealth, and power, there are also sad wishes. The suicide wishes for death. The angry person wishes for the destruction of others. The chroni-cally distrustful person wishes that others would do him harm so that he could justify his distrust.

Wishful hearing in everyday affairs gives an angry or cheerful tone to a neutral voice. It supplies words that were never meant to be there, and gives meaning that originates only in the listener's mind. Whenever what was heard is different from what was said, wishful hearing contributes this difference.

If you want to see wishful hearing in action, we'll eavesdrop on the following conversation between a salesman and a purchasing agent. The salesman works for a manufacturer and is trying to sell his product to this purchasing agent.

SALESMAN: You do like the quality of my product, don't you?

PURCHASING AGENT: Oh, yes. Your product is fine. But your competitor is lower in price. And in this product price is the thing that counts.

SALESMAN: Well, how much lower is my competitor?

PURCHASING AGENT: You know it's against policy to tell that, but they're definitely low. Besides, quality means very little in this case, as long as we have enough. Beyond that it doesn't matter. Your competitor has enough. Even if your quality were twice theirs, it wouldn't matter.

SALESMAN: Thanks. I see what you mean.

After the salesman leaves the interview he gives his own interpretation to the purchasing agent's remark, "Even if your quality were twice theirs, it wouldn't matter." He wires his manager the following: COMPETITOR SELLING AT HALF OUR PRICE.

Of course, the purchasing agent never said this. He gave no indication whatever of how much lower the competitor's price was. His remark which so influenced the salesman, might merely have been a way of driving home his point without really carrying any quantitative meaning.

But the salesman wanted to feel that he knew the answer. Perhaps he wanted to show how difficult the situation was. His wish to feel that not selling this purchasing agent was no reflection on his own ability caused him to hear what he wanted to hear.

4. UNWARRANTED ASSUMPTIONS. People who complain that

their lovers take them for granted may find some consolation in this: Most people take other people for granted. At least, they take for granted other people's knowledge and opinions.

There are too many gaps in the information which people exchange. This is a grand opportunity for wishful hearing to take over, supplying the information necessary to make the picture the way one wants to see it.

What's so golden about silence? It plays havoc in conversation, deceiving speakers and causing confusion. To the wishful speaker, his listener's silence implies understanding or acceptance or consent. The listener may really have intended none of these. He may not even have heard what the speaker said.

Don't make any assumption about what the other person knows. Fill him in. If you know from experience that he knows this, that's one thing. But if you just feel that he ought to know it and therefore leave it out of your talk, you can expect him to develop a picture different from the one you intended to convey.

In order to observe an example of one person having trouble getting through to another because of information left out, let's step into a doctor's consulting room. The doctor has just finished examining the patient. Let's listen in now.

> DOCTOR: You just have pharyngitis. An inflammation of the throat. Gargle three times a day with salt water and take some aspirin before going to bed. I'll also give you a prescription for some sulpha. Take the pills three times a day for three days. It's just a mild infection and I'm sure it'll be gone in a few days.
>
> PATIENT: Well, I'm glad to hear it's nothing serious. What causes pharyngitis?
>
> DOCTOR: Oh, some virus. You probably caught it from someone else who had it.
>
> PATIENT: Then I might give it to my husband or child. Should I stay away from them?
>
> DOCTOR: Well, you don't have to stay away from them, but don't get too close. Don't drink from the same glass or kiss them.

PATIENT: Do I have to boil the water before gargling with it?

DOCTOR: No, just use warm tap water.

PATIENT: How much salt should I put in a glass of water?

DOCTOR: Half a teaspoon.

PATIENT: I think that covers everything. Oh, yes, about the sulpha pills. Will they make me feel groggy?

DOCTOR: Chances are you won't feel them at all.

PATIENT: Just one more thing, Doctor. I know I'm taking up an awful lot of your time but is there anything I should avoid doing like taking a bath or eating certain foods?

DOCTOR: No, nothing special. Just take it a little easier. Get more rest.

PATIENT: Thank you, Doctor. You've been very kind. Shall I call you Monday if it isn't better by then?

DOCTOR: Yes, do that, Mrs. Harris. But I'm sure it will be.

If the doctor had put himself in the patient's place and visualized her going through the taking of pills and gargling, he could have answered all these questions in advance in his initial statement to her. It would also have been helpful to write out the instructions for Mrs. Harris. Even if she had had some experience with similar treatment before, she might have wondered what this particular doctor's views were on gargling and when to take pills.

How much simpler it would have been for both of them if the doctor had said something like the following:

DOCTOR: Mrs. Harris, you have pharyngitis. It's just a throat infection caused by a virus and should clear up in a few days. You probably caught it from someone else and to avoid passing it along, I would suggest that you not drink from the same glass or kiss any members of your family for the next few days.

Now, I'll write out the following instructions for you. Just gargle three times a day with lukewarm tap water containing a half teaspoon of salt in a glass of water. Also, I am going to give you a prescription for sulpha pills. Take three a day for the next three days whenever it is convenient for you during the day.

I would suggest that you take a pill around mealtime either before or after, as an easy way of remembering when to take it. If your throat still bothers you on Monday, call me, but I feel pretty sure you will be well by then. Is there anything else you would like to know?

5. HABITUAL SECRETIVENESS. There are people who keep a dark curtain over their mind and heart so that others cannot glimpse their thoughts and feelings. Such a person dislikes his own thoughts and feelings. He will also dislike anyone who has such thoughts and feelings. He expects, therefore, that if others knew his thoughts and feelings, they would dislike him and reject him.

To avoid such rejection he conceals this interior world. He feels that he is in the position of a suspect arrested by the police. He is warned that anything he says may be used against him. He is constantly giving himself this advice and following it, and therefore he says as little as possible.

Of course, this is an extreme case, but many people are counseled by an inner caution to conceal their thoughts and feelings to some degree. This varies with individuals. And one can find all shades of distrust ranging from the minimum, where the individual is completely open to others, to the person who puts the whole world under a cloud of suspicion and refuses to commit himself to anything.

Of course, it is often necessary to keep confidences for business or personal reasons. Nor is one expected to tell everything about one's self.

However, the habitually secretive person does not exercise discretion at all. The discreet person relies on his judgment to decide what he will and will not tell to various people. The habitually secretive person does not use judgment. He maintains secrecy no matter what he is talking about or to whom he is talking. He feels safer this way because for him any revelation seems dangerous.

Stop and think for a moment about how many secrets you really have. Suppose, for example, that you were to reveal to a neighbor or a friend some detail of your life which you had not originally intended to tell him about. Would something terrible happen? Could he use this against you and if he could, is he likely to?

In many cases you will realize that the feelings of anxiety you had about revealing this detail of your life were much greater than was warranted by the importance of the detail. Once you take a close, logical look at the situation you realize that these details aren't really secret at all in the sense that they must be kept. You do not need to reveal them if you feel more comfortable not doing so but you do not really need to worry about them coming out, either.

You might observe yourself in conversation. Do you ever tell things about yourself without being asked? When asked a question do you give just enough information to get by, or do you go beyond the question to give all the information the other person wants to know?

You would probably be surprised to note the range of communicativeness in people. Note their conversation and how little or much they are willing to tell. You will find that there is a habit pattern governing communicativeness.

In order to observe this pointless kind of secretiveness hindering communication, let's observe a personnel director interviewing a job applicant.

> PERSONNEL DIRECTOR: Now that you know something about the job duties and requirements, would you tell me about yourself? Let's start with your previous experience.
>
> APPLICANT: I worked in a department store and in a bank.
>
> PERSONNEL DIRECTOR: What kind of work did you do?
>
> APPLICANT: In the department store or in the bank?
>
> PERSONNEL DIRECTOR: In the department store.
>
> APPLICANT: I did selling.
>
> PERSONNEL DIRECTOR: What did you sell?

APPLICANT: Men's wear.

PERSONNEL DIRECTOR: Would you tell me a little more about the job?

APPLICANT: What do you want to know?

PERSONNEL DIRECTOR: Well, how long you worked at it, how well you did at it, how much you liked it? I would just like to know more about your experience.

APPLICANT: I worked there for two years and did fairly well. It wasn't a bad job.

PERSONNEL DIRECTOR: What about the job in the bank?

APPLICANT: That was while I was going to school.

PERSONNEL DIRECTOR: You mean you worked there part-time after classes?

APPLICANT: No, just summers.

PERSONNEL DIRECTOR: What did you do on that job?

APPLICANT: Messenger work, delivering mail, and I helped out with some filing.

PERSONNEL DIRECTOR: How did you feel about working in a bank?

APPLICANT: It was all right.

It is quite obvious that the applicant's secretiveness is self-defeating. He could have described his job in detail bringing out his duties, his reactions to the job, and how he feels this experience applies to the job he is presently seeking. But he probably felt he was safer saying as little as possible.

You Can Overcome Communication Blocks

Clear communication results in a meeting of minds instead of just an exchange of words; and a meeting of minds cannot be accomplished unless the human forces described in this chapter are dealt with. For these forces tend continually to pull a conversation off course. Two people in conversation can very easily move off in different directions and can soon be talking about different things. When this happens there is no longer a thinking together. Each person is pointing out his own problems and releasing tension, rather than working toward a common goal.

There are techniques for dealing with these human factors so that a meeting of minds can be achieved. These techniques are discussed in the following chapters. Acquiring skill in using them will require practice but this skill, once attained, will contribute immeasurably toward understanding others and having them understand you. Furthermore, using them skill-fully will help you to think straight and therefore to solve problems more efficiently. Let's get on now with the problem of how to talk so that you get through to others.

2

Encouraging Cooperativeness

Emotions Are Interwoven With Ideas In Conversation

Conversation is the main vehicle for expressing feelings as well as ideas. And since feelings are continually looking for outlets, we can see that conversations are bound to be filled with feelings, some erupting and others edging their way out.

Because feelings press for expression a person's talk often takes a tortuous course. He may interrupt the development of an idea to fume or gossip in order to unload a burden of anger. He may wander from the line of discussion to seek reassurance because of some anxiety. He may irrelevantly confess sins to relieve guilt, and expand on some pleasurable experience to share joy. He may stray from the point of the conversation to boast or to pity himself or others; to flatter or threaten; or to give praise, encouragement, or sympathy.

16

In conversation each person is pulled in two different directions: one is to develop a line of logic based on the facts brought out; and the other is to satisfy his emotional needs. Since he can only do one or the other at any given moment he has to do them alternately, and his ideas are usually separated by expressions of feeling rather than being linked to each other. The good conversationalist understands this need for venting feelings, allows for it, and shares in it.

As an example of emotional expression interwoven with pertinent ideas let's listen in for a moment on a business discussion between the sales manager and his boss, the vice president of marketing of a manufacturing firm. The company manufactures consumer products and sells them to wholesalers who in turn sell to retailers. The sales manager feels that the company ought to sell their products directly to the large retailers who are demanding this, rather than maintaining a policy of selling only to wholesalers.

> SALES MANAGER: I know we've decided not to sell any retailers direct but maybe we'd better take another look at this policy. I'm getting a lot of pressure from the fellows in the field. Some of the big retailers are threatening to cut down on our line unless we sell them direct.
>
> VICE PRESIDENT: We've got to stick to this policy, Bill. Our wholesalers will get pretty mad if we start taking their accounts away. And once we start with the big retailers the medium sized ones will get mad unless we sell them direct. It's your job to keep the field happy.
>
> SALES MANAGER: Oh, I can keep them happy, all right. You know that morale is pretty good among the men, and turnover of salesmen has gone way down since I became sales manager, isn't that so?
>
> (Here the sales manager has become anxious over the vice president's opinion of him and is looking for reassurance. The sales manager's bringing in evidence of his capability is irrelevant to the discussion and therefore must be motivated by some internal emotional pressure.)

VICE PRESIDENT: Oh, sure, I've got no complaints. Our main problem is to keep these big retailers in line. As soon as they get big enough to order in large volume they think they own you. They'd take the hide off you if you let them.

(This is a discharge of anger directed at the big retailers.)

SALES MANAGER: I've been telling the men to hammer away about our being presold through our big advertising campaign. And it's been working so far. But I've had to soothe a lot of irritated retailers. When I get in there myself they fall in line but the salesmen get browbeaten. The trouble is I can't be everywhere.

(The sales manager here is ostensibly describing the difficulty his salesmen are having. He makes the point that the retailers fall in line for him. This point isn't really necessary to convey the idea that the salesmen are having trouble. But the sales manager uses it as evidence of his capability to allay his anxiety. In effect, he is bolstering his ego.)

VICE PRESIDENT: Well, I guess you can't really blame the retailers. They're out to make as much as they can, just as we are. But we have to hold to this policy until we can think of something better.

(This is an expression of guilt over having angrily attacked the retailers in his previous speech. Here he takes back his attack.)

SALES MANAGER: OK, I'll keep at it. Say, I heard you caught a big one Sunday.

VICE PRESIDENT: Yeah. He really put up a fight. That was some of the best fishing I've ever had. (chuckles) My wife thought I'd landed a whale. Tasted good, too. Which reminds me, let's get some lunch.

(This is an expression of joy.)

Much of the feeling expressed by each person in a conversation is stimulated by the other person. Each reacts to the personality of the other and as a result is cooperative or resistant, friendly or hostile, praises, flatters, criticizes, reassures, gives or withholds information or expresses feeling in any other way available in the conversation.

Courtesy Encourages Communication

In any conversation, feelings influence thinking. Therefore, when you are trying to get your thinking through to the other person you cannot rely on logic alone. You have to encourage a feeling of cooperativeness in the other person.

If the other person feels uncooperative, he is likely to oppose you. This may be done in a number of subtle, elusive ways so that you can't directly criticize him for opposition although you are not getting from him what you want.

For example, he may withhold information, not by directly refusing to answer your question but merely by answering it in a non-illuminating manner. He may also neglect to mention information he knows you want but haven't thought to ask about. He may mentally withdraw so that he listens superficially but doesn't really grasp what you are saying. He may argue with you pointlessly, not to clarify thinking but just to place obstacles in your path. In the end he may reject everything you say, without even considering whether it makes sense, but simply because he wanted to reject you. And all this may be done with smiles and nods, and a superficial manner of agreeableness.

How are you going to encourage cooperativeness? Simply by being courteous. This means helping the other person gain something from the conversation. This gain need not be anything tangible but may consist of pleasurable feelings for him such as a feeling that you think well of his capability, appreciate any help he gives you, and respect his importance as an individual.

Three Ways Of Encouraging Responsiveness

Let's consider now three rules of courtesy that will encourage others to cooperate.

1. START YOUR CONVERSATION BY TELLING ITS PURPOSE. Two basic feelings in the other person that encourage his cooperativeness in conversation are: the feeling that he can trust you

and the feeling that you trust him. If he doesn't feel he can trust you he will not want to share his information and opinions with you for fear that in some way your knowing them might hurt him. His own internal police officer will warn him that anything he says can be used against him. As a result he will seek safety in reticence.

If he feels that you don't trust him he is likely to experience it as a blow to his ego, as an implication that he is untrustworthy. Your implicit attack on his character will cause him to resent you and therefore to oppose rather than to cooperate.

One common way of engendering distrust is to ask questions without telling why you want the information. When this happens the other person infers that you are not telling him why you want it because you don't want him to know why, because if he did know, he wouldn't give you the information or would act in some other way, contrary to your wishes. And, to reason further, since an individual generally acts in his own best interests, your withholding information to prevent him from acting in the way he would if he had such information, indicates that your best interests and his are opposed. This conclusion discourages cooperation on his part.

Too often, one person asks questions of another person in a conversation without giving the reason for asking these questions. As a result, the other person becomes suspicious. He feels that perhaps the first person is trying to trap him in some way. And often, the first person is. He purposely doesn't reveal his objective to prevent the other person from organizing contradictory arguments. The first person draws out information with which to build a case against the second person and then proceeds to corner the second person. However, the second person becomes wary after the first question and moves toward secretiveness, or defensiveness. In any case he is no longer trying to make sense but mainly wants to thwart you.

For an example of what happens when one person in a conversation doesn't orient the other person to the objective of the conversation let's listen to a discussion between a district manager and one of his salesmen. The district manager has observed that this salesman does not try hard enough to close the sale. The manager has not yet mentioned his observation to the salesman but intends to bring it out in this discussion.

DISTRICT MANAGER: Bill what do you think makes a good salesman?

SALESMAN: A good salesman? Drive, aggressiveness, being able to talk convincingly, planning his work. Why?

DISTRICT MANAGER: Do you consider yourself aggressive?

SALESMAN: Yes, I think so. You have to be aggressive to make sales.

DISTRICT MANAGER: What's your idea of being aggressive?

SALESMAN: Oh, let's see. Well, applying pressure, staying in the interview when it gets rough, asking for the order. (pause) I guess that's about it. But what are you getting at? Don't you think I'm aggressive?

DISTRICT MANAGER: What do you do in the sales interview?

SALESMAN: What do you mean what do I do? You've been on calls with me.

(Salesman is getting irritated)

DISTRICT MANAGER: I want to hear your view of it.

SALESMAN: I say, hello, present my product, show samples, give literature, and leave.

DISTRICT MANAGER: What about asking for the order?

SALESMAN: What about it?

DISTRICT MANAGER: Do you ask for it?

SALESMAN: Well, I wouldn't get it if I didn't ask for it, and you know my sales are moving up. You don't have any complaints about my sales do you?

DISTRICT MANAGER: Your sales are coming along fairly well but they could be better. On my last visit with you I noticed you didn't try hard enough to close.

SALESMAN: What do you mean? I try for a close in my own way. Each salesman has his own approach. You said yourself once we shouldn't use a canned approach

Anyway we happened to have a run of calls where the timing on many of them was wrong for closing. That wasn't typical.

In the above conversation the district manager was discourteous in that he showed distrust of the salesman by implying that the salesman would be dishonest about his own deficiencies. If we listen between the lines we can hear the following unspoken message of the district manager:

You're not interested in finding out the truth and improving yourself but only want to put on as good a front as possible and see how much you can get away with. You'll reject any constructive criticism I offer. You're untrustworthy in this respect and therefore I can't be straightforward with you but have to try to trap you into admitting your faults.

This unspoken message will come through to the salesman on an emotional level, as clearly as if it were spelled out. He may not stop to analyze that this is what the manager is implying but he will react emotionally with the same irritation. As a result the salesman will be motivated to oppose the manager as a way of expressing his anger.

We have here a situation where the manager has brought about in the salesman the very uncooperativeness that the manager was afraid of in the first place. The manager does not realize that he was responsible, through his tactlessness, for the salesman's resistance; and when he encounters this resistance from the salesman it only confirms to him that he was right in expecting opposition from the salesman and in trying to trap him into admitting his faults. This is the way a bad approach to people is perpetuated and is an illustration of why it is so difficult for people to change their ways of dealing with others.

Think of how different the discussion might have been if the district manager had opened with a statement like the following one: "Bill, I wanted to talk to you about the closing of the sale. From my last visit with you I felt that you weren't trying hard enough for a close. What's your feeling about this?"

The chances are that the salesman would have replied with something similar to the following: "I wasn't aware of this. I thought I was closing. Can you tell me specifically what you mean?" This should lead both of them toward getting down to specifics and taking an objective look at what was done as compared with what the manager thinks should be done.

2. RESPECT THE OTHER PERSON'S FEELINGS. In conversation many things are communicated that are not spoken. One of these is your attitude toward the other person. Through the way in which you listen to his ideas and explain your own, you let him know what you think of him.

For example, if you simplify your ideas so that a three-year-old can understand them, or over-elaborate on your instructions as though the other person were simple-minded, you are communicating a low opinion of the other person's mental ability. If you keep interrupting him you imply that you don't consider his ideas important enough to listen to.

On the other hand, if you share your feelings or confidences with him you are letting him know that you trust him. And when you ask for his opinions you are subtly complimenting him on his judgment.

Too often, people cull from their mental vineyard their choicest cluster of thoughts. Then they embellish this with polished words and spicy wit; but their thorny manner of presenting this choice message piques the sensibilities of the other person. Instead of receiving the expected admiration the speaker encounters sullen resentment.

No matter how brilliant or witty or logical your comments are their power is lost if they fall on a resistant mind. And one reliable way to induce resistance is to show disrespect.

As an example let's listen in for a moment on a nurse arousing antagonism in a patient.

NURSE: Good morning, Mr. Mason. How're you feeling today? Say, you hardly touched your breakfast.
PATIENT: I'm not hungry.

> NURSE: Not hungry! Mr. Mason, you'll never get well if
> you don't eat. Now let's try some of this cereal. It'll
> give you energy.
> (She ignores his feeling of not being hungry as though it
> didn't exist.)
> PATIENT: I don't want any cereal. I have a headache.
> NURSE: Am I going to have to coax you to eat? Here, I'll
> feed you this first spoonful and then you eat the rest your-
> self, like a good little boy.
> (Here she treats him as though he were a child.)
> PATIENT: I'll just have a little tea.
> NURSE: Just take one spoonful of this cereal. Come on,
> Mr. Mason, I've got lots of patients to take care of.
> (Here she implies that he is selfishly demanding all her
> attention.)

Although the nurse did not explicitly insult or attack the
patient she implicitly told him that what he said wasn't important, that he is like a child, and that he is selfish. How
could she possibly expect this patient to cooperate?

Let's look at how she might have handled it to secure his
cooperation. Suppose that the nurse has just commented to the
patient that he hadn't hardly touched his breakfast.

> PATIENT: I'm not hungry.
> NURSE: Tell me how you feel.
> PATIENT: I have a headache.
> NURSE: I'm sorry to hear that. I'll give you some aspirin
> for it and it'll go away soon. Meanwhile, I think it
> would do you some good to eat some cereal even if
> you're not hungry. How about it?

Here, the nurse has taken the patient's lack of appetite seriously, both by asking how he felt and by explaining why he
ought to eat even if he is not hungry. She has also considered
his headache and provided a remedy. Furthermore, she left it
to him to make the decision about eating, implying that he is
capable of making his own decisions.

When you are talking to others, practice thinking about what you are saying as though you were another listener. Ask yourself, How would I feel if this were said to me? What would I think of the speaker? How does he seem to feel about me? Would I feel complimented or slighted by what's being said? Putting yourself in the listener's position by asking yourself questions about how you would feel if you were listening to what you are saying will help you say the things that will encourage cooperativeness and diminish antagonism. It will sensitize you to hear between the lines.

3. ACCEPT IRRELEVANCY AND EXPLORE IT'S PURPOSE. Don't insist that the other person always remain relevant. With so many things to get done and so little time to do them there is a strong temptation to herd the other person's thinking so that he gets to the point as quickly as possible. It can be irritating to follow his apparently aimless wanderings into side ideas which seem to have no bearing on the issue at hand. But it's worth doing. For what's relevant to you may not be relevant to him and his apparent meandering might be a crucial link holding his attention to the conversation.

He may want to use the conversation for much more than arriving at a quick meeting of minds. He may want at the same time to tell you how good or smart or capable he is. He may want to find out what you think of him. He might want to release a little anger or anxiety or tell you how happy he is. Doing this may be more important to him than the actual subject at hand, and for him relevancy is determined by what he wants to do in the conversation rather than by its relationship to the subject under discussion.

You might say then that there are two kinds of relevancies: logical relevancy and emotional relevancy. Both of these determine whether an idea will be brought into a conversation and if you do not allow for his emotional relevancy he won't accept your logical relevancy.

It is basic in developing good relationships with others to keep in mind that conversation serves purposes other than the transmission of straight-line thinking. Conversation is a primary outlet for the expression of feeling and one must be flexible and patient enough to listen and respond to such expressions.

When a person introduces into a conversation an idea that is not logically relevant it does not mean that his thinking processes have gone haywire or that he fails to see the pattern of logic in the conversation. But there is a subterranean play of thought and feeling going on simultaneously within him. And whenever any part of this attains sufficient force he introduces it into the conversation.

Similarly, a silent preliminary activity goes on within a person when he suddenly initiates discussion of an idea. It seems to you as though he were just starting the discussion. But actually the discussion has been going on within his mind before his first remark and he is just bringing you into the middle of it.

As an example, take the following conversation between two friends, Jim and Paul. They are out to lunch together and are talking socially about the various things in their lives. There is a momentary pause in the conversation.

Jim is thinking about a camera he wants to buy that costs $100. He feels a little anxious about spending this amount of money for a camera especially since he and his wife have just recently been talking about their savings being on the low side and that they had better start tightening up their budget. Furthermore, he has a simple, inexpensive camera which has served its purpose over the years.

But the camera that he has seen advertised for $100 has so many attractive features, enabling him to get very unusual shots. He thinks with pleasure of the wonderful collection of striking candid pictures he could take of his children and of his wife and of the various events in their lives. Still, he feels bothered about spending the money and looks for some justification for doing it.

His mind travels back to the time when his children, aged

eight and ten, were babies. He finds that he scarcely remembers what they were like. He can't seem to construct a clear picture in his mind of their baby faces. If only he had more pictures of them.

He then thinks about the enjoyment he gets from taking pictures and wonders why he doesn't spend more time at it, or for that matter at any hobby. He doesn't seem to get enough real pleasure from his leisure time. He seems to be too pre-occupied with everyday business problems, with chores around the house, with taking care of the children. His leisure time seems to just fritter away in a television program here and a magazine article there, or mowing the lawn, or fixing the door, or talking over with his wife everyday things. There must be more to life.

At this point he gives voice to his feelings and says:

> JIM: You know, Paul, life seems to go by in a rush. I don't know where the time goes. It seems only yesterday that my kids were babies. I'm thirty-eight and I still feel like twenty-five. Maybe I'm not living enough, doing enough, getting enough out of life.

Remember all this started with Jim's conflict over spending the money for the camera. Without realizing it he's trying to convince himself that he ought to buy it. What he's really saying is that it's worth spending the money for.

Of course, Paul doesn't know anything about the camera but Jim's remark touches off in him a series of associations serving his own emotional needs. He is a little concerned that he isn't getting ahead fast enough in his job. He feels that he really should have a higher position. He uses Jim's statement to help himself feel more comfortable by making advancement seem less important. Let's listen to him do this and follow the conversation a little further.

> PAUL: You're certainly right about that, Jim. Before you know it it'll all be over. Maybe we knock ourselves out

> too much, trying to get ahead, when we ought to be try-
> ing to get a little more fun out of life.
>
> JIM: That's what I mean. You know, I don't even have
> a real hobby, something that would take me out of my-
> self, that I could really be proud of. You have to organize
> your leisure time or it gets wasted.
>
> PAUL: That's right. We drive so hard to get ahead that
> we forget that that's not the end-all of life. The im-
> portant thing is to be happy.

To a third person casually observing the above conversation
it would appear to be a philosophic discussion of the transience
of life, though the transience of life has little to do with the
real purposes of the conversation. Each person is merely using
this broad theme as a means of venting his own disturbing feelings without revealing the nature of these feelings.

Jim may not want to admit even to himself that he is con-
flicted over spending $100 for a camera. There may be factors
in the conflict that he doesn't want to face such as dependency
on his wife's approval of the purchase, having to be so concerned about a hundred dollars, and being afraid of acting im-
pulsively and regretting it. Paul, on the other hand, may not
want to face his own feelings of failure, much less admit them
to Jim.

The relevance of a remark depends very much on the personal purpose of the remark. In the above discussion the
personally relevant ideas were the conflict over buying the
camera and the feeling of inadequate progress in the job. The
idea actually discussed (the transience of life) merely provided
a common plane of interaction.

If a third person observing this discussion had tried to be of
help by bringing in comments of the great philosophers on the
meaning and purpose of life, which of course he would assume
to be highly relevant, he would merely have bored the first two
persons and soon lost their interest.

Relevance is determined by one's view of the purpose of the
conversation. But since any conversation consists of two or

more people, and therefore two or more views of its purpose, relevance is relative.

When the other person in your conversation brings in any idea that seems irrelevant to you it merely means that his purpose in the conversation is different from yours. Rather than dismissing his comment or pointing out its irrelevance it would be wise at this point to draw him out further to find out the purpose of his remark. Otherwise you and he are in danger of losing each other in the conversation.

As an example, consider the following conversation between a father and his twelve year old son.

> FATHER: Bill, from this report card you're not doing so well in school.
>
> SON: I know, Dad, but I really try.
>
> FATHER: I've been wondering about that. You never do any homework. You're always out playing ball or watching TV. You can't get decent grades without studying.
>
> SON: Well, Dad, I had it all worked out, about when I would study I mean. Remember we were supposed to go fishing last Saturday early morning. I was going to study all afternoon after we got back and then we were going to go to the movies in the evening.
>
> FATHER: What's fishing got to do with it?
>
> SON: Well, when we didn't go fishing it seemed to throw my whole day off. I didn't have any schedule anymore. I started doing other things and the next thing I knew the day was gone.
>
> FATHER: Now look, Bill, I'm not going to listen to any phoney reasons like that. You've got to learn to be responsible. Let's stick to the facts. Your grades are low and you're not studying. What are you going to do about it?
>
> SON: OK, Dad, I'll try harder.
>
> FATHER: I want to see you putting in some studying every day or you'll cut out the TV.

In the above conversation the father focused only on his own purpose of extracting from his son a commitment to study harder and achieve better grades. The son's introduction of the breaking of the fishing date did not make sense from his point of view. He regarded it as irrelevant. Certainly on the face of it the son's explanation seemed incongruous. Yet this very incongruity should have alerted the father to a need within his son which was pressing for expression.

By referring to the son's explanation as a "phoney reason" the father was blocking expression of this need and as a result discouraging cooperativeness.

Everything one says is relevant to one's own purpose and the fact that the boy introduced the broken fishing date indicated that he wanted to use the conversation for some other purpose. Let's take a look at what might have happened if the father had responded to his son's irrelevance by exploring it for the son's purpose. Let's assume the conversation began the same way and we enter it at the point where the son is explaining how the cancelling of the fishing date disrupted his day.

> SON: Well, when we didn't go fishing it seemed to throw my whole day off. I didn't have any schedule anymore. I started doing other things and the next thing I knew the day was gone.
>
> FATHER: Bill, I'm awfully sorry about the fishing, but your mother and I were out late Friday night and I was very tired. If you didn't study because of the fishing, it sounds like you're blaming me.
>
> SON: Not exactly, but this is the third time in a row you haven't done what you said you would.
>
> FATHER: It is? Let's see. I guess you're right. Looks like I haven't been handling my responsibilities well either. I guess you were pretty annoyed about the whole thing and it got in the way of your concentrating on your studies.
>
> SON: Well, I was pretty upset. Somehow I didn't feel like doing any homework.
>
> FATHER: I can understand that, Bill. Look, let's go fishing next Saturday, real early. I'll make it a point to get to bed early Friday night.

SON: Great!

FATHER: And, Bill, what about your studying? I know you were angry about the fishing but you're only hurting yourself when you get low grades. Even if I do the wrong thing in slipping up on my promises, is there any point in your doing the wrong thing by not studying?

SON: No, I guess not. I just wasn't thinking. I'm going to set aside a study period every day and stick to it.

Here the father widened the scope of the conversation to include the son's purpose as well as his own. The father did not decide what was relevant but accepted the son's relevance orientation as being as valid as his own. Having done this he encouraged cooperation by accepting both his son's resentment, and his own role in bringing about an emotional state that worked against studying. However, it was his acceptance of two orders of relevancy, his own and his son's, that enabled his acceptance of the son's resentment to come into play at all. Had he insisted on relevancy from his own point of view only, he would not have reached his son.

In your conversations practice listening for extraneous comments, for remarks that seem to be out of the order of logical thinking, and for the introduction of a topic by the other person where this topic is unrelated to anything that has gone before in the conversation. When you encounter this, draw the other person out. Try to find out why he really introduced the topic or made the remark he did. Doing this will make the difference between mere alternations of speaking and a close thinking together.

Cooperativeness in conversation is achieved when you show that you consider the other person's ideas and feelings as important as your own. Starting your conversation by giving the other person the purpose or direction of your conversation, governing what you say by what you would want to hear if you were the listener, and accepting his viewpoint on relevancy, will encourage him to open his mind to your ideas.

3

Drawing Out People's Thoughts

In dealing with the world each of us has a personal intelligence system for picking up information and interpreting it. Information is picked up through our senses—eyes, ears, nose, skin, muscles, and inner ear—relayed to our brain through the nervous system, and there interpreted. Our actions are then based on this information.

Much of the information we need is contained in the minds of other people. Sometimes they take the initiative in giving us information. At other times we have to draw it out.

Drawing Out Information Requires The Making of Demands

When you try to elicit information from someone, you are asking him to do something for you, to give up time and energy and possibly information that he doesn't wish to reveal, in order to organize a response to your request. You are asking him to lay aside his own thoughts in order to think about your ideas.

There are conflicting forces within the other person working both for and against giving you the information you want. Working against giving this information is his disinclination to be diverted from his own preoccupations. He has his own thoughts to think and his own ideas and feelings to express and he may not want to be bothered with answering your questions. Also working against his giving information is any feeling of secretiveness that he may have. He might feel safer withholding the information, feeling that the less you know about his thoughts the better off he is.

Working in your favor is his wanting an oportunity to express his ideas and feelings to another person. The feeling of helping you in some way may also encourage him to share information.

Make the Giving of Information Enjoyable to the Other Person

To encourage the giving of information you should make it enjoyable for the other person. Express your appreciation of what he is giving you so that he experiences more fully the pleasure of doing something for you. And listen with interest to comments of his which are not pertinent to your questions. If he expands on his answer, it is likely that he is enjoying venting his ideas and feelings. Give him the time and attention to enable him to enjoy this part of the conversation even though you may be impatient to get the information.

To show him that you are interested in what he is saying you can comment on it. Depending on the situation, you might express your sympathy, or tell him of some similar experience you had, or give him some information in return.

Sometimes, in his anxiety to get information an individual may impatiently pump another. For example, he may throw a series of questions at the other person, each question coming on the heels of the answer to a previous question. Doing this gives the impression of not considering the other person as having feelings and needs but merely as a source of one's own satisfactions; and in this case one's own satisfaction lies in getting the answers to certain questions. An individual with such an attitude is likely to treat the other person as though he were an answering machine.

Since each question is a demand that the other person provide information the person under cross-examination is likely to resent having a succession of demands placed on him particularly when he is given nothing in return. After a while each question is likely to be felt as a pin-prick of irritation, with each successive pin-prick becoming more annoying. This irritation is likely to move the other person towards warding off the irritating questions, much as he would brush away flies.

For an example of the unbroken-series-of-questions approach let's listen to Tom and Bill. They are at a party, having just been introduced to each other, and have been left alone to pursue their own conversation. Tom is curious about Bill and decides to satisfy this curiosity as directly as possible.

TOM: What sort of work do you do, Bill?

BILL: I'm a lawyer.

TOM: Do you specialize in any particular kinds of cases?

BILL: No, not exactly. Most of the work I do is in civil law, and I prefer that, but I handle some criminal cases, some divorce cases, and even some trusts and estates.

TOM: Where is your office?

BILL: At 500 Fifth Avenue. It's convenient to Grand Central.

TOM: Where do you live?

BILL: In White Plains. We moved up there from the city three years ago and the wife and kids love it. I don't like the commuting, but actually it's not so bad. I get a lot more reading done.

TOM: How long does the trip take?

> BILL: About an hour and ten minutes, door to door.
> It used to take me 25 minutes.
> TOM: How many children do you have?
> BILL: Two. A boy and a girl.
> TOM: How old are they?

Tom is preoccupied with acquiring information and probably doesn't notice that Bill's tone of voice is tightening with irritation. You may even be annoyed with Tom just from reading this. Bill, on the other hand, is distracted by the problem of how to extricate himself politely from this question-and-answer game.

Tom has completely lost his perspective on the situation. He sees only his own wish for information and is treating Bill as though he were an object to be examined and probed rather than as a person with needs and feelings of his own, which are just as important to him as are Tom's to Tom.

Other than the questions he asks, Tom is not participating in any way. He is not sharing his views, his feelings, his reactions to what Bill says, nor is he giving any information about himself. He is really treating Bill in the same way as he would an object. After all one puts questions to an object; not spoken questions, but questions just the same. One lifts an object to find out how heavy it is, feels an object to learn its texture, scrutinizes it for its appearance, and examines it in any other way to answer questions one has about the object. But one does not express views and feelings to the object nor share information with it.

In the above conversation Bill is not only made to feel like an object but is also deprived of any opportunity to satisfy his own curiosity about Tom. Furthermore, he is prevented from discussing subjects of interest to him at the moment which would give him an opportunity to vent his own views and feelings. He is kept too busy answering Tom's questions. And anyway he might be too polite to engage in a tit-for-tat, question-for-question sequence with Tom, or in a power struggle to control the course of the conversation. It is much simpler for Bill to just seek an exit from the conversation.

Tom's is an extreme case. But many people approach this extreme at times. And if it were less extreme, it would just be a matter of less alienation of Bill, but alienation just the same.

Tom should have kept in mind that Bill is a person and not an object, and that Bill would like Tom to share his views and feelings. Bill has his own curiosity about Tom and would like Tom to reveal things about himself. Tom's talking about himself would imply that he feels that Bill is someone worth sharing personal information with. Finally, Tom should have reacted in some way to Bill's responses, showing Bill that these responses made an impression on him.

Let's see how Tom might have handled the conversation if he were sensitive to Bill's existence as a person. We can see from this how Tom might have made the giving of information enjoyable to Bill so as to motivate him to continue doing so. This is fundamental to drawing out another person.

TOM: What sort of work do you do, Bill?

BILL: I'm a lawyer.

TOM: Well, I'm lucky to meet a lawyer at a party. They always have such interesting stories to tell. Do you handle criminal or civil cases?

(Here, Tom expresses a complimentary attitude towards lawyers before drawing Bill out further.)

BILL: Almost all of them are civil cases although I do still take a smattering of other kinds including criminal, divorce cases, and trusts and estates. I'm not really big enough yet to be fussy, or maybe I'm spending it too fast.

TOM: Well, don't be too hard on me, but I'm one of the guys that try to get you to spend it. I'm in advertising. An account executive with an agency. And from the looks of my low bank balance I really believe the stuff I put out. I guess we both fall into the pattern of what they're always writing about suburbanites, or aren't you one of us?

(Tom has anticipated Bill's curiosity by volunteering information about his own occupation and then goes beyond this by indicating that he lives in the suburbs and wonders if Bill does too. On the subject of place of residence Tom gives information on himself first. This willingness to share facts about himself encourages Bill to do the same.)

BILL: Oh, yes, I'm in the White Plains brigade in the battle of crab grass. And when I have bad dreams there's always a train in them. But the wife and kids love it, and I guess it's OK. But I feel disloyal to my commuter buddies if I don't complain a little.

In this conversation Bill is evidently enjoying himself, as indicated by the touches of humor in his remarks. Tom has revealed and shared something about himself, implying that he felt that Bill was a person worth sharing with. Tom responded to Bill's remarks, rather than just absorbing them, implying that he appreciated Bill's remarks and that they were worthy of comment. As a result Bill became more expansive. He felt comfortable in revealing his feelings and felt free to give information about himself. By sharing his feelings, giving information about himself, and commenting back on Bill's remarks, Tom diminished any initial resistance that Bill might have had to conversational engagement and opened wide the channel of communication.

Begin with Questions That Are Easy to Answer

When your primary aim in a conversation is to draw out information start by asking easy questions. Questions that are easy to answer relax the other person. People enjoy giving answers they know are right, and with easy questions you give the other person a chance to give right answers effortlessly. He begins by feeling this is going to be easy.

If you are a stranger to him he may start the conversation warily, feeling his way, wondering what you are like and what you want of him. He is on guard. He starts with whatever resistance and distrust is characteristic of him when talking to someone he doesn't know.

He wonders, Will you be difficult or easy to talk to? The first things you say to him create an impression that answers this question for him. If you make it difficult for him he becomes evasive and withdraws. This in turn may cause you to press harder which continues a vicious cycle by driving him away still further.

If on the other hand you start with an easy question, his tension begins to dissolve. You are not so difficult to deal with, after all. He answers the question with confidence. You ask him another easy question. He relaxes still more and his answers flow out more easily. He is getting used to talking to you. He is already engaged in conversation.

For example, a lawyer interviewing a witness should start off by asking such simple questions as what time of day the incident happened and where the witness was located at the moment rather than immediately asking the witness to describe the event.

Similarly, a manager interviewing an applicant for a job ought to begin with such simple questions as: Where do you live? and, Are you married? Then the interviewer can launch into such searching questions as: Would you tell me something about your past experience? or, Why do you want to work for this company?

A real estate agent, confronted with a prospective purchaser of a house, can start the conversation rolling by asking about such easy things as the kind of house the prospect lives in now, and the time it takes him to get to work, rather than leading off with a question about the kind of house the prospect is looking for.

First, you have to warm the conversation a bit so that when the other person dips in to feel the temperature, he is encouraged to plunge.

Structuring Questions

Now that you have made the other person comfortable in the conversation, how do you put your questions in order to get full and accurate information?

One useful way of classifying questions is by their degree of structure. The structure of a question has a great deal of influence on the kind of answer given. A highly structured question asks for a specific fact. The question specifies that the answer must lie within a closely circumscribed range. For example, if I asked you what time it is, the structure of the question limits the answer to a specific time of day. Or, if I asked you, Do you like strawberries? I expect an answer that indicates whether or not you do. There may be further qualification on your part, but these are not required by the question.

This kind of question, calling for a specific answer within a very restricted range of possibilities, is a highly structured question. Here, a structure of ideas has been fully developed in the question. The person answering has very little thinking to do, little thought-structure to formulate. He merely has to respond with a fact.

A low-structured question, on the other hand, requires little thought to formulate it. It is designed merely to stimulate the other person to talk in a particular area, without the questioner necessarily having much of an idea about where the talk might lead. Here, the structure is in the answer rather than in the question. For example, some unstructured questions might be: Why do you want this job? and, How do you think you might improve the situation?

Of course, a question is not necessarily either a high-structured or a low-structured one. There are all degrees of structure. For example, the following series of questions starts with a very low-structured one and moves progressively to more structured ones: How do you feel about work in general? How do you feel about your job? How do you feel about your supervisor? Do you like your job? The first three questions are of relatively low structure, with each one becoming a little more structured than the preceding one, since it narrows still more the area of discussion. The last question is of high structure since the other person can answer it with a yes or a no.

Since high-structured questions require little thought on the part of the other person they are easier to answer. All the thinking is done by the questioner. Therefore, as described earlier, it is best to begin a conversation with high-structured questions to make it easy for the other person to enter the conversation. Once he is immersed you should move to low-structured questions in order to find out what lines of inquiry to pursue with more structured questions.

As an example of the use of structured and unstructured questions to get the fullest and most accurate picture of what's in the other person's mind, let's watch a doctor talking to a patient who has just come in to see him.

DOCTOR: What seems to be the trouble?

PATIENT: I've had a pain in my stomach for the past few days and I thought I'd better come in to see you about it.

DOCTOR: What kind of a pain?

(Here the doctor continues with another unstructured question in an attempt to draw out a general picture of what's in the patient's mind. This is better than moving immediately to such structured questions as, Have you had any fever? or, Did you feel nauseous?)

PATIENT: It's sort of a sharp pain. I notice it particularly after I eat.

DOCTOR: Are there any particular foods that seem to cause it?

(Here, the doctor has moved to a more structured question. He wants more specific information now in order to establish a tentative diagnosis which can then be evaluated through tests.)

In the above example, if the doctor had started immediately with highly structured questions, he might not have gotten the information he needed to start him thinking in the right direction. His gathering of information would have been done on a trial-and-error, hit-or-miss basis and he might have had too many misses before he struck a hit. Such questioning can lead to hasty, unfounded conclusions and often represents a leaping for quick answers.

Another example of the use of structured and unstructured questions in securing information, is the following conversation between a job interviewer and a job applicant.

> INTERVIEWER: Why do you want to get into selling?
> (Unstructured question.)
> APPLICANT: I like working with people and trying to convince them about something.
> INTERVIEWER: Well, that's certainly needed in selling but there are a lot of other things too.
> (Although this is not in question form it has the effect of being a question if the interviewer pauses after he makes this statement. Also, it is unstructured, merely prodding the applicant to talk some more about his reasons for going into selling.)
> APPLICANT: Well, I know you have to be aggressive and there is a certain amount of travelling involved. I like that, too. I like being out and getting around. Also, I feel that selling is one of the best ways to get ahead in the company.
> INTERVIEWER: In other words, selling is really a stepping-stone to a management position.
> (Again, although this is not in the form of a question, it has the effect of a question since the interviewer stops and waits for a reply from the salesman. Also, it is a structured question, asking for a specific commitment from the applicant. Actually, the interviewer wants to evaluate the interest the applicant really has in selling. Is he really interested in working at selling or is he trying to find a quick way to a management position?)

Essentially, low-structured questions are used for the following purposes: to get a general idea of the direction of the other person's thinking; to find out things in his mind which you might not have thought to ask about specifically; to get at feelings which might not be revealed in answer to a specific question; and to draw the other person more actively into a discussion.

High-structured questions on the other hand are used: to obtain specific facts; to check your thinking against the other person's to make sure that both of you have the same concept in mind; and to get the other person to commit himself to a definite position.

Techniques for Drawing Out Information

The key to effective drawing out of information is the low-structured question. This type of question requests the other person to talk about a particular topic rather than merely provide a specific fact. It sets the other person's mind actively in motion since the other person has to organize structure in order to answer. And once his mind is set in motion the momentum carries him forward, often farther than he originally expected to go. In other words, people are often reluctant to start talking and then when they do start, are just as reluctant to stop.

Many people are more bothered by telling half of the truth than by not telling any of it. Once they have been coaxed into giving part of the picture, they are unable to leave it that way. They seem to be afraid that the other person will get the wrong impression from part of the picture. As a result, they feel obliged to complete it.

The more unstructured the question, the more information you are likely to get. As a result, in a conversation in which you are asking a good many unstructured questions, the other person is likely to be doing most of the talking. And this is as it should be when you are drawing out information. In fact, you can check the effectiveness of your drawing out by comparing how much he is talking with how much you are.

Four Ways of Asking Unstructured Questions

Let's consider now some ways of asking unstructured questions.

1. ASK QUESTIONS THAT CAN'T BE ANSWERED BY YES OR NO. One of these is asking questions that require an explanatory answer. In order to answer your question the other person must explain what he means rather than merely provide a fact, or a yes or no.

Some examples of unstructured questions are as follows: What do you think of this policy? How do you feel about making the changes? What happened? Why did he refuse? Unstructured questions generally call on the other person to explain how or why, or ask him to describe something.

Questions involving when and where are more highly structured. Another kind of high-structured question is one which gives the other person two or more possibilities and merely asks him to make a choice. For example, the question, Do you like this? merely asks the other person to choose between yes and no. Similarly, the question, Which of these three do you like best? merely asks the other person to pick one of three given items.

2. PREFACE KEY WORDS WITH "WHAT ABOUT" OR "HOW ABOUT". A second way of asking an unstructured question is prefacing the topic word or words with the phrase, What about, or How about. For example, asking, What about transportation? or, How about the accommodations? is another way of requesting the other person to start at some relevant point and explain about transportation and accommodations, respectively.

3. REPEAT BACK THE KEY WORDS. A third technique for employing the unstructured question is repeating back the key word in the other person's previous answer. For example, when you ask another person how he felt about his last job and he

replies that he liked it pretty well but had trouble with the boss, you might draw out more information by responding with, "Trouble with the boss?" Here, you are merely repeating back some of his words, implying that you would like to know more about it. Or, as another example, if the other person says to you, "You've got a good product there but it's not economical," you might draw him out further by responding with, "Not economical?"

4. SUMMARIZE BACK. A fourth way of drawing out information falls somewhere between a structured and an unstructured question approach. This is to summarize back to the other person your understanding of what he meant. If he agrees, it becomes a structured question to which he merely says something equivalent to yes. But if he disagrees, he is faced in effect with an unstructured question where he has to explain the basis of his disagreement and give you another explanation of what he means. Often, the other person will add new information.

As an example, let's consider a discussion between Tom and Joe where Joe is resisting doing something that Tom wants him to do. Joe feels that it costs too much. Tom might then summarize back to Joe as follows:

"Joe, let me see if I understand correctly what you mean. You like my idea and would go ahead with it but you don't want to spend this much money now. Is that right?"

Joe might merely reply, "Yes, that's right." Or he might say, "Yes, that's the main reason," implying that there are other reasons that Tom can pursue. In this case Tom, by summarizing, has at least drawn out a lead to a further line of inquiry. As a third possibility, Joe might reply:

"Yes, that's right. And anyway I don't know how the people around here would take to your idea. And I've got to work with these people."

Here, Tom, by summarizing, has actually drawn out another reason for Joe's unwillingness to go along with his idea.

As a way of reviewing some of the ideas discussed in this chapter, let's take a look at them in action, in the following discussion between two managers.

JIM: Frank, I'd like to talk to you about this supervisor position we have open. I was thinking about Bob Brown for the job. Do you think he'd be interested in it?

(Here, Jim opens the discussion by stating its purpose and starts off by asking an easy question.)

FRANK: Yes, I'm sure he would. He's eager to get ahead.

JIM: How do you think he'd do in the job?

(Jim asks an unstructured question, requiring an explanatory answer.)

FRANK: Well, I don't know. He might do all right. He's smart and aggressive. Gets the job done. Of course, I don't know how well he'd get along with the people under him.

JIM: Get along?

(Jim draws out further by repeating back some key words.)

FRANK: Well, Bob's a little too self-centered. Always has to be right. Doesn't look at the other person's side enough.

JIM: I'm glad you brought that out. It's certainly important for a supervisor to listen to his people and understand their problems. How do the other men in his group feel about him?

(Here, Jim first comments back on Frank's answer as a way of avoiding a cross-examination effect. He then asks for information through an unstructured question which is likely to draw out more information than would a structured form that requires merely a yes or no, such as, "Do the other men in his group like him?")

FRANK: They think he's bright and capable but he rubs them the wrong way. I don't think they'd want him as a supervisor.

JIM: Then you feel that all things considered we shouldn't take a chance on him?

(Jim summarizes back Frank's feelings as a means of getting either a definite commitment or more information.)

FRANK: Well, I'm not saying that exactly. He's a good worker and he's got the brains for the job. In fact, we don't get men with his capability that often. Maybe we ought to consider this further. We might be able to make him see the importance of considering the feelings of others. If we handled him right and gave him some special training maybe he'd grow into the job.

JIM: That sounds like a good idea. Makes a lot of sense. Thanks for your help, Frank.

In order to learn to use these techniques skillfully you're going to have to practice them. Get into the habit of applying them in your conversations. It may seem awkward at first but with continued use they'll go more smoothly. As a result, your conversations will be more enjoyable and more productive.

4

Dealing with People's Emotions

Emotions Move Us Toward Self-Expression

Emotions are essentially motivators. They are forces prodding us to action. Things happen around us or within our bodies, and in response to these things we feel emotion—anger, fear, joy, guilt, shame, envy. Emotion is experienced as tension; and since tension is generally unpleasant we are moved to act in a way that will remove the tension.

Emotions help the individual to cope with his environment; for his desire to lower the tension moves him in the direction of greater safety or comfort. For example, fear is felt as an unpleasant tension. The individual wants to get rid of this unpleasant tension and learns that he can do so by avoiding some danger that threatens him. By making people unpleasantly tense, fear moves them to run from danger which in turn makes for survival.

47

Similarly, anger is felt as another unpleasant tension which occurs when one experiences something blocking his way to a desired object. He gets rid of this unpleasant tension by destroying the obstacle and achieving his goal. Anger causes him to fight to get what he wants when not getting this might mean hurt or death.

Even joy insists on expression. People feel uncomfortable when they have to contain it. They want to shout, sing, jump, or at least talk about it.

Emotions push us to do something to remove the tension they cause. And one of the commonest ways of removing tension is through talk. Direct action as a way of expressing emotion is often unsuited to civilized society. As a result conversation is not only a method for communicating ideas but is also the dominant outlet for emotions. In order to deal more effectively with emotions in conversation let's consider first how they operate.

Emotional Reactions Depend on What's Happening Within the Individual

The emotional reactions of an individual to a specific situation cannot be predicted. One cannot say definitely that an individual will be angry because the circumstances call for anger, or that he will be joyful, anxious or guilty because he is supposed to be. One person may become quite angry in the exact same situation that another accepts with equanimity. Similarly, where one individual reacts anxiously another may feel quite secure. Furthermore, the same individual may react differently to the same situation at different times.

The reason for this variation is that emotional reactions are caused by factors within the individual as well as by external ones. Since the internal factors vary from individual to individual, and from time to time in the same individual, emotional reactions will vary even when the external situation remains the same. For example, any trivial annoyance will arouse more anger in the hungry man than in the satisfied one.

There are no rules to guide an observer in making a prediction of how another individual whom he does not know well will react emotionally. Of course, this does not mean that emotional reactions occur at random. There is an ultimate orderliness to the occurrence of emotions; but since any rule would have to be based on both internal and external factors and since the casual observer seldom has access to the internal factors, he is generally unable to predict how an individual unknown to him will react emotionally.

Let's take an example of an internal factor causing anger. Frank is having difficulty in making a decision. He goes to Bill for advice. Bill's advice is unacceptable to him. Frank would rather do something else and had hoped that Bill would advise him to do what he wanted to do. When Bill suggested a different course of action Frank got angry and justified this anger by imagining that Bill doesn't really care about him but only thinks of himself.

Actually, Frank was really angry at his own inability to make a decision and his dependency on Bill to help him make it. Rather than face the uncomfortable idea that he is dependent, Frank lets his anger out at Bill.

You cannot logically expect another person to get angry simply because factors are confronting him that in your view should make him angry. He isn't necessarily going to get angry at the same things that make you angry. Conversely, you cannot predicate on a logical basis that another individual should not be angry when he is angry. Just because it appears to you that there is nothing about a situation that should arouse anger in him doesn't mean that he won't be angry for his own reasons. The same holds true for other emotions such as fear, guilt, and joy. As long as we can't see another person's inner world—and we generally can't—we can't be sure how he will react emotionally in any given situation.

You need only gaze for a moment at your own inner world of fantasy to realize what continual and varied activity goes on there. In connection with these fantasies there is a constant play of emotions which often bears little relationship to the events around one. Think of the daydreams in which you heroically triumphed, revenged yourself on someone you feel has hurt you, or were mistreated by someone you fear. How much of this fantasy life really comes true?

How often have you found yourself overly anxious about some trifle when you knew that so much anxiety wasn't warranted; yet you couldn't shake it? Can you remember ever being excessively angry over some little pin prick of annoyance which perhaps at other times might have been shrugged off? Haven't you on occasion felt elation sweep through you even though nothing particularly wonderful had happened?

The truth is that all the unwarranted worry or anger could not have been caused by the trifle. *Emotions are always proportionate to their real cause.* The trifle became only an excuse for being anxious but there must have been some event occurring in your inner world that was proportionate to this amount of worry.

Let's take an example. Suppose that Dick and Paul work for the same company on the same level and that a vacancy has occurred in a higher position. Both of them are eligible for this opening and want it. Each is competing with the other.

In a conversation with his superior Dick makes a remark that he later realizes could be interpreted as putting Paul in a bad light. Dick becomes very anxious that he has done something wrong, something that will harm his friend, Paul. In reality the remark might have been harmless, having no effect on the superior's impression of Paul, and was not even necessarily interpreted by the superior as being critical of Paul. Nevertheless, Dick feels very uncomfortable, much more worried than the remark justifies.

This unwarranted anxiety might be caused by Dick's unconsciously wanting something bad to happen to Paul to put Paul out of the competition for the promotion. Having this un-conscious wish makes Dick uncomfortable even though he is unaware of the wish. He is anxious that he might act on it, doing something that will hurt Paul. However, he is aware only of the anxiety, and not of the real reason for it.

Dick has repressed his wish to hurt Paul, experiencing only the acute anxiety. The anxiety is so high because it is pro-portionate to the act of hurting Paul and not to the remark. Since Dick is not conscious of his wish to hurt Paul he thinks the anxiety results from the remark he made. He dimly realizes perhaps that the remark does not justify so much anxiety, yet he is not able to find any other explanation for it.

Emotions Are Displaceable

The non-rationality of emotions results from their being dis-placeable. In the example given earlier in this chapter where the dependent individual resented the other person's advice, anger was being displaced. The dependent individual was really angry at his own dependency but removed the focus of his anger to the other person. Similarly, in the later example, Dick attributes his anxiety to his remark to his superior about Paul, rather than facing his unconscious wish to hurt Paul.

The displacing of emotions is actually an act of concealment. It is like the feint of the magician when he makes a diverting gesture with his right hand in order to draw the audience's attention away from his left.

In the case of emotion the individual is both the magician and the audience. He wants to conceal from himself some un-pleasant aspect of his inner world. When there is a threat that this unpleasant aspect will suddenly be illumined by the harsh glare of an emotion he shifts the spotlight of the emotion to some object outside himself. His attention becomes focused on this external object and the real cause of the emotion re-mains in the dark.

Why Logic Won't Dispel Unwanted Emotions

Since emotions are displaceable logic won't help in getting rid of undesired emotion. After all, what is the point of showing someone the illogic of being angry or anxious about something when that thing isn't really the cause of the anger or anxiety? You wouldn't be doing anything to alleviate Dick's anxiety about his remark to his superior by telling him that such an unimportant remark isn't any cause for such anxiety. The remark wasn't even the real cause.

To draw an analogy, let us suppose that a man refuses to go out in a canoe with you because he can't swim and is afraid of drowning if the canoe should tip. At the same time he doesn't want to admit to you his inability to swim. So he says instead that he is afraid of catching cold if the canoe tips. You can readily see that your reassurance to him that the water is warm and that therefore he need not fear catching a cold would in no way lessen his anxiety about going out in the canoe.

The only difference between this case and the case of Dick's anxiety about his remark to his superior is that Dick was not aware of the real cause of his anxiety. Therefore, if we want to make the analogy complete, all we have to do is suppose that the man who refuses to go out in the canoe is unaware that he is afraid of drowning but really believes that his fear of catching cold is his real motivation for avoiding the canoe trip.

It is futile to try to dissolve fear or anger in another person through logic. Emotions simply are not responsive to reason. In fact, reason is likely to intensify an emotion. When you apply reason you make the other person feel irrational in expressing his emotion and thereby block him from doing so. This blocking increases his tension which only makes him experience the emotion more acutely.

Yet people are so terribly tempted to rely on logic to dissipate an unpleasant emotion in another person. The other person's attempts to justify his emotional reactions are so transparently illogical that one can hardly help feeling that it takes but a word here or there to set the other person's thinking straight.

One is also tempted by the delicious opportunity to be right which can do so much to make one feel clever. The only trouble is that the other person is not at the moment receptive to logic. Besides which, your logic isn't even valid since it's not based on the real reason for his emotional reactions but on the reason he gives.

If you have ever tried to talk someone out of a fear of the dark, or of water, or of dogs, or of anything else, you must have experienced the uselessness of logic in dealing with emotions. Still it's difficult to resist trying, for faith in the power of logic to control human reactions dies hard. But the next time you encounter an emotional reaction in someone and find yourself reaching for some piece of logic to dispel his emotion, give it up. It won't work anyway and it might only worsen the situation.

How to Deal with People's Emotions

What then should you do? Four ways of dealing with emotions are discussed below.

1. ENCOURAGE EXPRESSION. Since emotions produce tension and press for release, in order to diminish the tension the first thing to do when encountering emotion in another person is to encourage its expression. There is little point in trying to get anything across to him since in his heightened state of tension the other person will be too distracted to think about what you are saying. In fact, he isn't likely to even listen. No matter how sensible an answer you have for him, hold back on it. Concentrate instead on getting him to talk.

Let's take an example. A supervisor assigned one of his subordinates to handle an unpleasant task. The supervisor picked this particular subordinate because at the moment he was the most readily available and also because he showed particular skill in handling this type of problem.

The subordinate responds as follows.

"I'm getting fed up with always being given the dirty assignments. How come you always pick on me when something unpleasant has to be done? What am I, the low man on the totem pole around here?"

The supervisor knows that he hasn't given more nasty jobs to this fellow than to the others. The supervisor might be tempted therefore to confront him with the fact of equal distribution of unpleasant tasks. He knows he's right and the subordinate wrong and he might therefore feel that all he has to do is introduce this piece of information and the subordinate's anger will evaporate.

Such information is only likely to make the subordinate still angrier. From his overall relationship with his superior the subordinate knows whether or not he is treated fairly. He has some idea about whether he is being assigned a disproportionate amount of dirty jobs. And even if this were so—although in this case we are assuming it isn't—why should the subordinate become angry now? Why couldn't he merely state his protest in a calm manner?

He could, if he weren't angry at something else. Perhaps he is angry at his wife or at himself or at his superior for some other reason and this request triggers off his anger. The anger presses for release, and given what seems like a justification the subordinate expresses it.

At this point the superior should encourage this expression. He should try to get the subordinate to talk further. He could ask the subordinate, "Why do you feel I am picking on you?" and the conversation might continue as follows:

> SUBORDINATE: Well, when a lousy job has to be done you're always putting the finger on me. Hell, I don't mind it once in a while, but this is getting to be too much.
>
> SUPERIOR: You feel that I don't give the other fellows dirty jobs also.

(Here, the superior continues to draw out the subordinate and at the same time tries to get the subordinate to clarify his position.)

SUBORDINATE: Oh, they get a nasty one handed to them once in a while, but I seem to be the prize patsy around here.

SUPERIOR: I didn't know you felt that way.

(The superior is again encouraging further expression first, by not attempting at this point to refute what the subordinate is saying, and second, by implying that it is a good thing that the subordinate is expressing himself since it is enlightening the superior.)

SUBORDINATE: Well, I don't like to gripe, but I think this is going too far. I'm not saying you haven't been pretty good about most things but this assigning of dirty jobs isn't working out right.

(Having let off the initial blast of anger the subordinate is beginning to subside, to view the situation more rationally. He is starting to show a little more perspective on the situation when he points out that the superior has been fair about most things. His mind is opening and the superior can now start introducing the facts.)

SUPERIOR: I can understand your being annoyed if you feel that I'm throwing all the rough jobs at you, but actually this isn't the case. This time you were the only one available. Let's take a closer look at what has been happening in the past.

(The superior could then lead the subordinate through a discussion of the frequency of unpleasant tasks assigned to him as compared to his co-workers. Here, the superior would get down to specifics.)

It doesn't matter what the emotion is. As soon as you encounter it, stop presenting your reasoning and concentrate on the other person's emotions. Focus on getting him to talk.

If he's worried about his health, or about losing his job, or about what someone thinks of him, or about anything else, don't give him reasons why he needn't be worried. Your reasons aren't likely to have anything to do with the real sources of his worry. All they do is stop him from talking because now he has to listen to your explanations of why he shouldn't worry.

Instead, ask him to tell you a little more about it. For example, if he tells you that he's worried about an operation he has to have, it's pointless to tell him not to worry, that it's a simple operation. Instead, ask him to tell you what led up to the decision to operate. In explaining this he will be releasing his anxiety. After he talks about it for a while you can give him some reassurance such as telling him what you know about this kind of operation. You might comment on how others were worried beforehand about a similar operation and it turned out to be easier than they expected.

If someone is worried about losing a job, or that someone else doesn't like him, don't immediately tell him that he doesn't have anything to worry about, that he's doing a good job or that you're sure this other person does like him. Instead, ask him to explain why he's afraid of losing his job or what makes him feel the other person doesn't like him.

Similarly, if a person tries to express joy by talking about his children or grandchildren or about a happy time he has just had, ask him to tell you more about it. Be careful not to take the conversation away from him by starting to talk about your happy times or by changing the subject.

You may become impatient at listening to the other person's expressions of feeling but taking the time to do this is well worth while. It will result in better communication and more satisfying personal relationships.

2. MAKE THE OTHER PERSON AWARE OF HIS FEELINGS. Our emotions are a valuable part of our equipment for enjoying life, giving color to it. But because they distract attention they often interfere with the transmission of ideas from one mind to another. Getting the other person to express his emotions, as described earlier, is the primary way of dealing with them. But sometimes this is difficult because the other person lacks conscious awareness of what he is really feeling at the moment. This combined with an unconscious desire to conceal the emo-

tion both from himself and from others, works against his expressing himself. It may make him secretive, or he may express anger in the disguised form of sullen uncooperativeness.

When you find this happening you have to make the other person aware of what he is feeling. You can't do this by merely telling him that he is angry or anxious since he is only likely to deny it and perhaps to become irritated, since he doesn't want to believe it. Rather than telling him directly what he is feeling you should first suggest that his behavior seems to indicate that he has this feeling; that having this feeling is quite understandable and acceptable; and that you'd just like to know more about it so that perhaps you can help. In short, you've got to get him talking about what he's feeling. When you have done this he is likely to become aware of his feelings.

Emotions can hide in our unconscious, motivating us without our being aware of them. A person may act on his anger without realizing that he is angry. He may be anxious or guilty without knowing it other than perhaps experiencing a vague discomfort.

Man's prodigious intellect, which has worked such technological wonders, has also served him in developing ingenious ways of disguising his feelings to hide them from himself.

For example, the same anger that loudly announces its presence through violent actions or harsh language, can sneak out as gossip, as destructive criticism, or as teasing. Other common ways of releasing anger are through uncooperativeness and argumentativeness.

In addition to its direct expression, anxiety may be expressed by overcautiousness, by excessive talking about a particular subject, or by secretiveness. Withdrawal and avoidance are other ways of expressing anxiety

Guilt is frequently expressed through self-criticism, confessionals of real or imagined misdeeds, and through acts of atonement. And apart from the obvious expressions of good cheer, joy is released through references to pleasurable experiences.

Let's take an example of how to deal with a disguised emo

tion. Suppose a salesman finds himself confronted by a buyer who is uncooperative. He is reluctant to talk. The buyer merely replies laconically to questions as though he were impatiently waiting for the interview to run down.

The buyer's unwillingness to enter into the conversation very likely is an expression of anger. He knows that the salesman would like at least some information. His refusal to cooperate must stem from some sort of resentment. If he were acting on purely rational considerations, he would at least tell the salesman that he can't give him any information.

Since the salesman is unable to get the buyer to release his anger through talking, the salesman should try to make the buyer aware of his own feelings. To do this the salesman has to get him to focus his attention on his feelings. The salesman can't very well tell the buyer directly that he is uncooperative and that this uncooperativeness arises from some hidden anger. However the salesman can subtly draw the buyer's attention to his own feelings by saying something like the following:

> Mr. Jones, I wonder if I or my company has in some way offended you. I get the impression that you are irritated with us for some reason since you don't seem to want to discuss the product. If this is the case, I would appreciate your telling me so that we could do something about it.

This kind of remark is likely to cause the buyer to examine his own feelings for a moment to see whether or not he is annoyed. He will want to find out why the salesman got this impression. In so doing the buyer may realize that he is angry and that this anger is causing him to treat the salesman discourteously.

If the buyer is really angry at the salesman or his company, he is likely now to tell the salesman why. In so doing the buyer will be releasing his anger. The salesman can help this along by drawing the buyer out further. This should help clear the air, enabling the conversation to proceed more smoothly, with greater involvement of the buyer.

If, instead, the buyer is angry at something else and is letting it out on the salesman, he will come to realize what he is doing. As a result of becoming aware of his discourteous treatment of the salesman, through no fault of the salesman's, he is likely to soften in his approach and come out of his shell to meet the salesman half way.

Now, it is quite possible that getting someone who is angry or anxious to focus on his feelings will yield nothing but a denial, and continued opposition. But one has nothing to lose and everything to gain by trying this.

3. ACCEPT EMOTIONS WITHOUT CRITICIZING THEM. When a person expresses emotion, particularly if he expresses it strongly, he often becomes anxious about doing so. He is afraid that the emotion will get out of hand, that he will lose control of himself.

In our unconscious are often basic impulses towards pleasure, urges to get what we want when we want it, and to destroy what stands in our way. These were there from birth, and in infancy we acted directly on these impulses, not caring about others. As we grew up we learned to adjust, to compromise, to consider the needs of others, to wait for something if we couldn't have it immediately. We even took pride in our ability to master these impulses and to cope constructively with the problems of reality.

However, many people, to varying degrees, feel these raw impulses strongly and have little faith in their ability to master them. As a result, they become frightened that some impulse will get out of control and that they will do something harmful. When they express an emotion intensely they wonder anxiously, Am I losing my grip, my hold on reality?

Some people who have this chronic fear play safe by holding back their feelings, allowing very little emotion to be expressed. Others, after expressing intense emotion, take it back, trying to undo what they have said.

As an example of the taking back of emotion let's listen for a moment to an angry man denouncing his tailor to his wife because the tailor did not deliver the man's suit when it was promised.

"That stupid, lousy tailor was supposed to have my suit here yesterday. It's still not here. How the devil does he expect to run a business when he can't get anything delivered on time? (pause) I was counting on that suit. (pause) Oh, well, maybe it wasn't his fault. He's probably crowded up with work or his delivery boy got sick again."

After his initial blast of anger the man became uneasy and tried to erase his attack on the tailor by providing reasons why the tailor didn't deliver. It is likely that the vehemence of his emotion, which was after all disproportionate to his inconvenience, frightened him and he back-tracked.

Another device one uses to reassure himself that his emotions are under control is to compare himself with others to make sure that he is not different. For example, when asked why he is worrying so much over some little thing, a person might respond with a remark such as: "Wouldn't you be worried if you were in my position? or, "I don't think I worry more than most people over this kind of thing."

While any emotion when felt intensely may cause anxiety concerning its control, anger is a particularly disturbing emotion in our culture. We seem to be brought up to be frightened of anger either in others or in ourselves. We seem to be anxious that something dreadful will happen as a result of it. This probably results from an intimate association in our minds of anger with violence.

Consequently, husbands and wives are afraid of each other's anger; subordinates fear their boss' wrath; salesmen are frightened that their customers will be irritable; and in general people quake inwardly at the prospect of encountering temper. People will often submit to demands, giving up doing what they wanted to do, just to avoid arousing another person's anger.

The important thing to keep in mind about anger is that it is a completely natural reaction of the body. When one wants something badly and can't have it, or is hurt in some way, he generally gets angry. Anger is as natural a reaction as is breathing or salivating or excreting. It generally doesn't result in violence at all. Violence as a consequence of anger is the very infrequent exception. If violence or anything drastic resulted whenever anger occurred, mankind would have perished long ago. The fact is that when anger is around it is generally either controlled, or released in some momentary outburst. It then subsides, and the usual course of events is resumed.

The way to make a person comfortable whenever he expresses intense emotion is to accept it without judgment or condemnation. Never point out that he ought not to feel a particular emotion. The fact is he does feel it and he can't control the way he feels.

Emotions are not controllable. One can control what one does about the emotion, but the experience of the emotion itself can no more be controlled than can the secretion of gastric juices or the circulation of the blood. Therefore, if you tell a person he shouldn't feel the emotion, he may become frightened that he is losing control, since he may mistakenly think that he should be able to prevent feeling it.

When he is angry or anxious tell him that you can understand his feeling that way about the particular situation. This does not mean that you agree with the arguments he brings up. You are really implying that there is nothing for him to worry about in having these feelings even if you don't necessarily agree with the points he makes.

For example, suppose a customer is angry at a salesman because of a late delivery of merchandise and expresses this anger as follows:

"How do you expect me to do business with your company when you can't even get the merchandise here on time! You're messing me all up. Can't you people organize things any better than that?"

The salesman should first express his understanding of the customer's anger before discussing the facts. He might reply as follows:

"Mr. Smith, I certainly can appreciate your being upset about our late delivery. I know it can cause you an awful lot of trouble, and I'm terribly sorry about it."

The salesman can then go on to draw out the buyer's anger further by exploring with him how late the delivery was, what trouble it caused, and what the salesman can do about it to rush some merchandise there.

After the buyer's anger has subsided as a result of talking it out, the salesman might ask him to consider their past record of delivery, assuming this is good, as a way of pointing out to the buyer that lateness is infrequent and that the feeling of disorganization that the buyer has about the salesman's company does not match the facts. Presenting these facts should be done only after the buyer has calmed down. If he is still angry, your logic will only block further expression of his anger, which will make him angrier.

Get into the habit of searching your feelings. Admit them to yourself as much as possible and accept them. Don't judge them morally any more than you do your nose or hair. When you do admit and accept them you will be much better able to control your behavior. If you deny these emotions you are likely to act on them without knowing that they are motivating your actions; and you might do things you will later regret.

In general, bring feelings, both yours and others, out into the open as much as possible. When the other person is in an emotional state get him to talk about how he feels and about what seems to be causing it. Similarly, when you feel agitated find an opportunity to talk out your feelings.

Emotions operating within us magnify the importance of the subjects they focus on; and, like shadows in the night, these subjects loom large and frightening. But when emotions are brought out into the clear light of reality by talking about them, the subjects they are focusing on assume their true proportion. Talking about feelings not only diminishes tension but enables a more realistic appraisal of a problem.

5

Listening Between the Lines of Conversation

Explicit and Implicit Messages

Each line of conversation conveys several messages simultaneously. One of these messages is communicated through the meaning of the words. This is the explicit message. Other messages are transmitted *by implication*. These we shall call *implicit* messages.

The individual's implicit messages express his real feelings or the things he really wants at the moment. Therefore, to understand an individual by knowing his likes and dislikes; to cultivate a relationship with him by giving him what he really wants; to protect him from what he wants but shouldn't have; and to influence him by relating your ideas to his interests; you have to listen between the lines and deal with his intentions.

This requires cultivating the habit of continually analyzing motive. What does the speaker mean besides what he is explicitly saying? How does he feel? What does he want? And usually you have to hold up your end of the conversation while answering these questions for yourself. With practice it will become second nature and you will be much better able to achieve a meeting of minds.

Let's take an example. Suppose you are sitting on a park bench on a warm, sunny, Summer day. A man who is a stranger to you shares this bench. Both of you have been sitting there silently.

Suddenly he remarks, "Beautiful day. Hardly a cloud in the sky."

The explicit message in his remark refers to the beauty of the day and the absence of clouds. But he is also communicating implicitly. For one thing he indicates that he wants to have conversation with you. Secondly, by choosing a very conventional, impersonal opening he conveys a wish to be at least moderately proper about opening conversation with a stranger. After all, he could have opened a little more brashly with, "I had a delicious bowl of beef stew for lunch," or "What do you do for a living?" or "My name is Frank Williams, what's yours?"

You reply, "Yes, it is a beautiful day. If I had known it was this warm, I wouldn't have worn my coat."

Your explicit message communicates that you feel the day is beautiful, that you hadn't realized before coming out that it would be so warm, and that you regret wearing your coat. Beyond this is your implicit message which tells that you are willing to talk with him, and that you would like to carry the conversation even further since you introduce a more personal note, your regret about wearing your coat.

Now suppose he replies in turn, "I don't blame you for wearing it, though. It is a very good looking coat."

Beyond his explicit message that he considers your coat good looking he is also communicating the following implicit messages: he *wants you to know* that he considers it good looking, which very likely indicates that he wishes to please you; he would like to continue the conversation; and he feels that even if you knew the weather were warm you might be motivated to wear the coat because of its fine appearance.

The context of a remark determines the implicit messages it conveys. For example, in the above conversation the words themselves of his opening remark about it being a beautiful day do not imply a wish to engage you in conversation. It's only as an opening remark that they contain this intention. If instead these words were a reply to a question the implicit message would change while the explicit still remains the same.

The explicit message might be defined then as the content of a remark completely apart from its context. The implicit messages come from the total context.

To illustrate further, suppose someone in your family enters your house and seeing that you are about to go out, comments that it is raining and that you had better wear your rubbers. In addition to telling about the rain he communicates that he thinks you don't know it is raining, that he cares about keeping you from getting wet, and that he feels that he can influence you.

Implicit messages can be communicated through the pacing of ideas and the timing of pauses as well as through the words. For example, in conversation, overelaboration or repetition, which slows the pacing, implies that the speaker is anxious that he is not getting his ideas into the mind of the listener. Ironically, his over-explaining often brings about the result he dreads—the listener's tuning out because he feels that he already knows what the speaker is saying, had grasped it the first time, and can afford to not listen to the unnecessary repetition.

Similarly, with regard to pauses, a listener may realize that he has the answer to the problem the speaker is posing, before the speaker stops. In his eagerness, the listener then replies with his answer just as the speaker finishes his last word. This gives the speaker the impression that his ideas were not thought about, carefully considered; that the listener was just waiting for him to finish so that the listener could have his say.

Generally, in conversation when ideas are being exchanged

there is an instant's pause between a comment and a reply to the comment. This is part of the rhythm of talk and is the time needed for the listener to absorb the comment and formulate at least the opening of his reply. When the ideas presented are difficult to absorb the pause is longer. But when there is no pause at all, it implies a lack of thought or even of listening.

Therefore, when you reply in conversation make sure to pause for the instant even if you've already formulated your reply. This courtesy of implying that the other person's ideas deserve consideration, will help cultivate his receptivity to your ideas.

Expressing Unacceptable Desires

As illustrated above, we are continuously communicating through two channels—explicit and implicit. But why do we need two channels? The answer is, because we are civilized.

Living in a society requires that we abide by a whole complex of rules—legal and moral laws, family and community customs, and etiquette. Since these rules are man-made we are not born with natures that are inherently fitted to these rules. This means we must continually make compromises between what our natures want and what the rules require.

The ability to compromise, to give up part of what he wants, develops as the child grows. The little infant has no scruples. He tries to get what he wants in any way he can. As he grows older he learns that he must not kill, hurt, cheat, steal, lie, or be discourteous. He comes to know the penalties for each of these—penalties imposed not only by others but by his own conscience as well.

But human nature is alive and kicking within him. He wants, yet has to curb many of his wishes; he gets angry, and at the same time must control his temper; and he gets frightened, but hides his fear when it seems shameful.

This vital, energetic, demanding human nature won't be still. It insists on a voice. But because men's minds are atuned to the Rules this voice of primitive impulse would sound offensive and even threatening.

As a compromise, therefore, the channel of implicit communication is used. What is proper is said explicitly. What might offend is implied.

By implication we can praise and reassure ourselves; insult, reject, and derogate others; talk about the things we want but shouldn't really ask for; and tell others that we like them where shyness prevents a direct declaration. We can also attempt to control others through threat or flattery while claiming innocence of such discourtesy.

Implicit Communicating In The Five Major Interpersonal Operations

This all really comes down to the following five interpersonal operations: 1. building up one's self; 2. attacking others; 3. making demands; 4. controlling; and 5. expressing love.

Let's take a look now at the use of implicit communication in each of these operations.

1. BUILDING UP ONE'S SELF. Insufficiency of self-confidence seems to be a very common ailment. So many voices are saying, explicit or implicitly, look at me, see how clever, handsome, brave, strong, funny or virile I am. See how much I have and how much I know.

Some voices are blatant. Others, in deference to a code of modesty, appeal indirectly for praise.

The implicit appeals for approval are by far the most common. Only those very hungry for praise resort to boasting. For boasting incurs disapproval—the very opposite of what the boaster wants.

Let's take a look at some subtle forms of self-praise. Between the pressure of self-doubt on one hand and our subscription to humility on the other we have developed a fairly high degree of skill in this art.

In the following example Harry is talking to his wife, Jane.

HARRY: That story I told last night sure had them laughing. It's good to have a few stories ready for a party but you have to know which ones to choose to fit the group you're with.

(Here, Harry is praising himself for his skill in telling stories that make other people laugh and also in selecting stories that are effective with a particular group.)

JANE: It's a funny story and it always pulls a laugh, but did you see Dick's face and the way he and Gwen looked at each other?

HARRY: Oh, them! I don't think they know the facts of life. Some times I wonder how they had kids. Well, you can't please everyone and I'm certainly not going to worry about what they think. Do you really think the story bothered them?

(Harry is asserting his independence by claiming a lack of concern over the opinions of others. At the same time he expresses anxiety about Dick's and Gwen's opinion when he asks if Jane thought they were really bothered by the story.)

JANE: Oh, they were bothered all right. I'll hear about it in my next conversation with our hostess.

HARRY: Why does she invite people like that to this kind of a party? If you want a party to be a success you have to pick your people carefully. You have to know what they like and don't like. Remember that surprise party I made for you last year? Why do you think that was such a success? Because the people really fit together well, like pieces in a jig-saw puzzle.

(Harry acclaims himself a capable planner of parties and astute judge of people.)

In the above dialogue Harry never praised himself explicitly. He never said, "I am a good story teller," or directly asserted that he is clever in planning parties or a perceptive judge of people. But certainly the implications are obvious.

Let's take another example. Tim and Larry, fellow employees, are talking.

TIM: What did you say to the boss, then?

LARRY: Well, I said that I know this is an important job but if I'm going to take responsibility for it I have to do it my way. I didn't want there to be any misunderstanding later. I believe that you've got to say what you think no matter who you're talking to.

(Larry is showing how independent he is and how unafraid of authority.)

TIM: How did he react to that?

LARRY: Oh, he agreed. He knows my work. Of course I told him that if I needed help I'd certainly come to him because I valued his experience and his sound advice. You've got to make people feel important. You get further with them that way.

(Larry points to the boss' high opinion of him and to his own shrewdness in handling the boss.)

Larry, like Harry in the previous example, never directly praised himself. Nevertheless, the facts were presented so that they reflected credit on him.

When a person says, "I'm smart," he's obviously bragging. But he can imply the same thing merely by describing a difficult problem that he solved. Since the problem requires smartness to solve, the listener must draw the obvious inference.

Similarly, a person indirectly indicates his own bravery by describing a dangerous mission; points to his virility or attractiveness by narrating his sexual conquests; demonstrates his strength and skill by performing or telling about a particular physical feat; displays his erudition by reference to obscure facts; and indicates his access to celebrities through name-dropping.

Such implicit self-praise reflects a need for reassurance. The individual is trying to convince both you and himself that he is adequately endowed with the characteristic referred to. To make him more comfortable—and thereby more receptive to your ideas—tell him that his action certainly indicates the presence of that characteristic. And if you feel that he particularly is strong in this characteristic, you can embellish your reassurance.

However, don't stray from what you feel is the truth or he will come to distrust you. For deep down he knows what is true. Even so, he may very well under-rate himself, thinking himself less bright, generous, attractive, or capable than he really is. And when he implicitly seeks reassurance to raise his low opinion of himself, you can ease his tension for the moment by responding with praise.

2. ATTACKING. Words can be fashioned into devastating weapons. They can be quite painful psychically unless one is sufficiently self-confident to be impervious to their sharp edges. Unfortunately, few of us are self-sufficient enough to be completely indifferent to insults and critical remarks.

To varying degrees most of us are affected by what others think of us. We inflate with pleasure when we are praised and bristle with anger or shrink glumly when we are insulted or criticized.

The bludgeoning verbal attack is explicit. When someone curses, or namecalls, the anger is obvious. There is actually less pain in such an attack, for the very excitement in the attacker undermines the credibility of his remarks. What he says in the heat of anger isn't to be taken seriously.

The cutting remark made calmly is more wounding. The explicit message—the words themselves—may sound like objective criticism while the attack is implicit. It has an air of rationality and truth about it. And the more angry the victim becomes, the more the insults seem to fit.

Four forms of those implicit verbal attacks are: a) unfavorable comparison; b) minimizing (including faint praising and pointed remarks) ; c) teasing (which includes ridiculing and sarcasm) ; and d) gossip. Let's take a closer look at these.

a) UNFAVORABLE COMPARISON. The unfavorable comparison is done *explicitly* by comparing two people with regard to a particular characteristic, pointing to the presence of it in one person and the absence of it in another. It is done *implicitly* by merely emphasizing to the person under attack the presence of a desired characteristic or the absence of an undesired one, in the favored person.

Let's take an example. Suppose a man arrives home late for dinner and finds his wife angry because he hadn't telephoned to let her know.

She says, "Why didn't you call me? Now the dinner is ruined. Here I've been waiting for you and worrying and everything is spoiled."

He replies, "I'm sorry, honey. I had some last minute things I had to take care of at the office. Some people phoned just as I was leaving and then I had to get some letters out. Anyway, I'm sure the dinner is fine."

She's still angry and says, "Maybe it's fine for you but it isn't for me. All the joy of cooking is lost when the food is spoiled. Other men call their wives when they're going to be late. They're considerate."

Here, the wife not only stuck in the knife, but she twisted it. She started with a thrust at a particular point—his inferior judgment about telephoning. Then she widened the wound by characterizing him as inconsiderate. This is, in effect, a personality interpretation that would cover a wide range of behavior. It would tend to bring up in him any anxiety he might have about being inconsiderate.

Similarly, a supervisor may implicitly criticize an employee who has just spent five days on a particular task, by saying, "Joan finished this kind of problem in three days." A doctor may hurt a patient who is protesting about the discomfort of a particular treatment, by saying to her, "My other patients don't complain about this treatment." And how many of us have winced at hearing a mother say something like this to her little daughter: "Look at your dress. Mary's mother tells me that Mary never spills any food on her clothes."

Unfavorable comparisons are particularly painful because comparing one's self favorably with others is a common way of reassuring one's self that one is a normal, capable, or worthwhile person. Being different can be frightening. It tends to stir up self-doubt.

When someone in a moment of anger interprets your personality unfavorably to you or compares you as inferior in some respect, it means that he is reaching for a verbal weapon potent enough to match his rage. He knows that this sort of attack is likely to be particularly hurtful since he is thrusting at a vulnerable point—your feeling of adequacy, of worthwhileness as a person, your measuring up to the other fellow. And few people are secure enough in their self-esteem not to be bothered by such a stab.

When you are the target try to keep in mind that very likely the other person is letting out anger from other sources, taking out other frustrations on you. And his words do not really represent his opinion of you but merely reflect his anger of the moment. It would be best to keep him talking so that he vents his anger as much as possible. Don't ignore his attack for this will only increase his anger. At least be concerned that he is angry even if you aren't bothered by his slights.

When you are the angry one avoid interpreting personality or comparing unfavorably. You can blow up as vehemently as you wish about the particular action that offends you but confine your attack to the incident rather than generalizing about the person.

b) MINIMIZING. Minimizing other people's efforts as a way of belittling them can be done very subtly, often without the belittler being aware of what he's doing.

I remember being utterly dismayed at a program chairman's comment to the audience after the first speaker had finished. The speaker had talked for about three-quarters of an hour. The chairman first publicly thanked him and then implicitly dismissed his speech as worthless by remarking to the audience, "I'm sure we all enjoyed that talk very much. It can be summed up in the following sentence." The chairman then went on to give a summarizing sentence thereby implying that the three-quarters of an hour spent listening to the speaker was wasted since one sentence would have done the trick.

Another example of minimizing is when you go all out to do something superbly or to give someone a special treat and the only comment you get is something like, "You ought to do this all the time," as though it were that easy.

Damning with faint praise is really another form of minimizing. How do you think a woman feels when she has just had her hair done, puts on a new favorite dress, and grooms and paints and shines herself until she feels that her radiance must make the room glow, and her husband's only comment is, "You look all right."

Her feeling would probably be similar to that of a man who had just made his lowest golf score in ten years. In response to his excited announcement he hears from his wife, "That's nice, dear."

The pointed remark is a variation on faint praise. Here, one not only weakens the praise by qualifying it, but suggests deficiencies in other areas. For example: "He's a nice fellow when you get to know him." Does this mean that he's not nice at first?

"She dresses well when she has a date." Does this imply that she's slovenly when not dating?

When you are giving praise give it wholeheartedly, unreservedly. Be definite about it. Often people have mixed feelings about something because they like some aspects of it and dislike others; and they seem to average their feelings as though this average were a true representation in a single expression. This expression comes out as weak praise.

The listener, however, interprets the faint praise not as a combination of likes and dislikes but as a general lack of enthusiasm about all aspects.

Therefore, when you do have mixed feelings don't give one comment to express this mixture. Separate these feelings. Praise unstintingly the aspects you like and criticize just as freely the parts you dislike.

c) TEASING (INCLUDING RIDICULING AND SARCASM). Teasing, ridiculing and sarcasm are other methods of mounting an implicit verbal attack. They are disguised expressions of anger.

Teasing looks to the casual observer like playful humor. And it certainly may have humor in it and be quite amusing to anyone watching it. And under certain circumstances a person being teased may even be grateful for the attention. Nevertheless, the person doing the teasing is attempting to provoke the other. Similarly, ridicule and sarcasm are aimed at belittling, at making someone feel foolish.

For example, a girl shows off a new evening dress and someone says, "That's a very pretty nightgown." A man proudly presents a new car he just bought and a friend comments, "Your car looks in good condition. I know where you can get the best trade-in on it if you want to buy a new car." A child sings a song and a listener remarks, "That's a nice poem you recited. I bet if somebody added some music it would make a pretty song."

In the above examples the teaser implies in the first case that the evening dress looks like a nightgown; in the second case that the car seems used; and in the third case that the child can't carry a tune. If the teaser had said these things explicitly he would obviously be attacking. Saying it implicitly through teasing doesn't change the fact of attacking. It only means that the teaser has some anger to discharge without having any way of justifying the anger. So he lets it out through teasing. And if the teasing is clever, there is also the pleasure of being witty.

This exposing of teasing, ridicule and sarcasm as muted expressions of anger is in no way intended as a criticism of them. After all, anger is a natural part of human functioning. There is nothing evil or wrong about anger. And it is healthier to express it. Why not then spice its expression with humor and wit? Think of how delightfully Cyrano's nose is ridiculed! Consider how entertaining mimicry can be!

These displays of wit are certainly much more in line with man's artistry and intellect than are screaming, cursing or physical violence. Suppose a man trips and falls. You ask him if he's hurt. Admittedly a gracious reply on his part such as, "No, thank you," or "Yes, I am a bit," would be nicest. But after all the man is annoyed for having fallen. Isn't it much more pleasant to hear from him something like, "No, I'm just down here to do push-ups," even if it is sarcastic, than to listen to him say, "Yes, you stupid fool. Don't you think it hurts to fall?"

If teasing is a part of the way you relate to people, there is no need to give it up. You enjoy it, and if it's done artfully, others probably enjoy it, too. And it is harmless. But do it in moderation.

When you are being teased try to avoid reacting angrily or hurtfully. This kind of reaction will tend to point out implicitly to the other person that he is really attacking you and it will make him uncomfortable with you.

d) GOSSIP. And what's wrong with a little gossip? It's generally another harmless way of venting irritation. Of course, slanderous gossip can destroy reputations. But most gossip is merely a chewing over of information about someone's faults, where opinions aren't really changed anyway; and a little steam escaping eases internal pressure.

For example, suppose two fellow employees, are talking about a third.

"Looks like Mike is on the carpet again. The boss sent for him about an hour ago."

"What can you expect. That guy is always in someone's hair. He's never on time and he talks your ear off."

"Yeah. The other day he was telling me about some smart investment he made. I thought he'd never stop talking."

"If the boss doesn't watch out, Mike'll be telling him off."

"I try to avoid going to lunch with the guy. It's no good for my digestion. He really gets me mad the way he's always got to be right. Nobody else knows anything."

Now what harm does that really do Mike? The other two both feel this way about him anyway and all they're doing is giving each other a chance to let out a little anger.

When you find yourself gossiping to someone about the shortcomings of another person there's no need to feel contrite, to condemn yourself for talking about someone behind his back. Little private gossip sessions are a harmless way of letting out irritation. As long as you're not deliberately trying to set other people against someone but are just sounding off spontaneously to ease your feelings, have a good time. The chances are you're not really hurting anyone.

3. MAKING DEMANDS. An *explicit* demand is made by directly asking for something. The *implicit* demand stops short of this. Instead of asking the other person to do or give, the implicit demand merely states what one wants. One then relies on the other person's desire to please.

Let's take some examples. If a woman says to her husband, "I'd love to go to the theatre Saturday night," the chances are that her husband hears it as, "Take me to the theatre Saturday night." She hasn't explicitly demanded this but the expression of her wish combined with his desire to please is experienced by him as a demand that he take her to the theatre.

When someone conducting an interview gets up from his chair this is an indication that the interview is over as far as he is concerned. His rising is an implicit demand that the other person leave. Another way of making this demand is to ask, "Is there anything else you'd like to talk about?" The implication is: If not, then the interview is over.

Interrupting another person in a conversation constitutes an implicit demand that he stop talking and instead listen. Conversely, if you remain silent instead of continuing a going conversation, after someone has answered your question, you are implying that you want him to elaborate further.

An implicit demand can often be made quite gracefully. One can get what one wants and at the same time give the other person the pleasure of granting fulfillment of a wish, rather than merely the feeling of submitting to a demand. Asking someone to grant fulfillment implies that he has a choice. Demanding submission leaves him no alternatives. In the interview example above, rising leaves no choice, while asking if further discussion is desired allows the other person to decide.

When making demands, be explicit. People generally prefer to be asked for something directly. If you make your demand implicitly you may actually stimulate resistance to your demand as a result of the other person's resentment at your not asking for what you want in a forthright manner.

While implicit demands can be made gracefully one has to be careful about doing this; and implicit demands always allow the other person to avoid complying by deliberately misinterpreting your wish. And of course he may really misunderstand while you may at the same time grow annoyed at him because you feel that he is intentionally refusing you.

However, when someone makes an implicit demand on you treat it as an explicit demand. First make it explicit by feeding back to him your understanding of what he wants, and then tell him to what extent you are ready to comply. Don't ignore it by pretending not to have understood that he was implying a demand, since he will assume you have understood and are purposely denying him what he wants.

4. CONTROLLING OTHERS. A common way of trying to control others is by exploiting their dependency on having the esteem of others. The one seeking control promises approval for compliance and threatens with disapproval for opposition. This granting or withholding of approval can be done implicitly merely by saying something like, "If I were in your place this is what I would do," and then telling the other person what is wanted of him.

Offering the approval of others as a reward is done when an art dealer says to a prospective purchaser of a painting:

"I bought this painting from a friend. He hated to part with it. And I suspect that a good part of his love for it was inspired by the enthusiasm of his guests. They were all very much impressed by this painting."

One can readily imagine the image developing in the prospective purchaser's mind of his guests clustering around the painting as it hangs in his living room. They admire the artistry and thereby indirectly, the good taste of their host.

Here the art dealer attempts to control the purchaser by appealing to his desire for other people's approval.

People are often influenced because of their self-doubt. They worry that they're not smart, virile, brave, kind, generous, strong or healthy and seek ways of proving to themselves that they really are. To motivate, the influencer may offer reassurance for the particular anxiety as a benefit of complying with his demands.

For example, to one who is unsure of his own judgment, the influencer trying to sell an idea might say, "It seems to me that this would be the smart thing to do now." To one anxious about his kindness the influencer might say, "It seems to me this would be the considerate thing to do at this point." In effect, the influencer is implying that by performing the suggested acts the self-doubter will demonstrate that he really is smart or kind. Ironically, the self-doubter's very susceptibility to this kind of manipulation indicates that he feels a lack of these desired attributes.

When someone suggests that you do something, note whether a judgment of you in some respect is incorporated in the suggestion, whether it be his judgment or the judgment of others. If such a judgment is implied, separate this from the suggestion itself so that you can decide on its own merits the worthwhileness of doing what he suggests. On occasion, you may want to follow the suggestion for the considered purpose of impressing someone. But at least you will be doing this deliberately, rather than being manipulated into following the suggestion by a fear of being undesirable in some way or by the illusion that it will make you better.

5. EXPRESSING LOVE. The word love, perhaps more than any other, has a different meaning for each individual. For some it is a feeling of wanting to possess. To others it means submission. Still others equate it with sexual excitement. And some think of it as giving.

Perhaps it would be presumptuous to offer a categorical definition of something that for centuries has occupied so much of the thinking of poets, philosophers, theologians, and psychologists. We shall, therefore, talk about it merely in the way we mean it, as it is expressed in conversation. Perhaps a useful conception is that talk expresses love whenever it is not being used to build up one's self, nor to attack, nor to make demands, nor to control.

The sheer pleasure of talking with someone whose company we enjoy, of sharing our feelings, of indicating respect for the other person's likes and wants, and of pleasing the other person for its own sake are all expressions of love.

For example, you express love when you listen to someone's troubles and try to make him feel more comfortable; when you compliment a person, not to gain some advantage, but just to give him pleasure; when you give advice to be helpful and not to control; when you accept another person's anger without attacking him in return, not because you are afraid of him, but because you want him to feel comfortable in releasing his feelings; and when you give information in order to be helpful, and not because you want something in return.

When hate is removed one just naturally loves. As a parallel to this, when one is not praising one's self, nor attacking, nor demanding, nor controlling, one is expressing love in conversation.

Practice Listening Between the Lines

Acquiring sensitivity to the implicit content of conversations requires practice. When you listen to others talking or are engaged in conversation yourself, get into the habit of asking yourself, Why is he saying this? What is implied?

When there is a suggestion to think or act in a certain way, observe whether some pressure is exerted by implying that noncompliance indicates a deficiency in intelligence, appearance, generosity, bravery, honesty, or social acceptability. Your awareness will help you separate the pressure from the merits of the suggestion.

Note the requests for praise in the telling of incidents that in some way reflect credit on the speaker. Watch for exhibition-

istic displays of erudition or wit. Both the telling of such incidents and the exhibitionistic displays are bids for praise. And
if you want to please the other person, give him the compli-
ments he wants, if you feel they are deserved. He will appreciate your sensitivity to his needs and your willingness to
satisfy them.

Sarcasm, ridicule and teasing should be quite obvious. Keep
in mind that these are disguised or toned-down expressions of
anger and are coming out in this way because the speaker would
feel too uncomfortable letting his anger out more directly. If
you can, view these expressions as an attempt by the other
person to ease his tension, and accept them without retaliation,
and if you wish, play along with them. Observe also the sharing and giving.

Gradually greater sensitivity should come. And with it will
also come greater effectiveness and pleasure in conversation.

6

Giving and Getting Feedback Of Thinking

The Same Words Stimulate Different Mental Images

Man's superior intellect enables him to compare objects and separate out the aspects they have in common. For example, he can see that an orange, a tennis ball and the moon have in common that they are round; that a banana, a steak and a piece of cheese resemble each other in that they are edible; that water, glass and air are similar in that they are transparent; and that roses, fire engines and blood are alike in that they are red. This ability to compare, to separate out common elements represents an advance in intellect of man over the animals, and is not present in children until several years of age.

The ability to separate out aspects or common elements is the basis for language, since each word stands for a common element or pattern of common elements. For example, the word, *ape*, stands for all creatures having certain anthropoidal characteristics in common. The word, *soft*, refers to the quality of yielding under light pressure no matter in what object it is found.

Each word, then, might be considered a generalization. The word chair, for example, covers all kinds of chairs—bridge chairs, easy chairs, stools, beach chairs and swivel chairs. Therefore, when someone says to you, "I bought a chair," you know very little about his purchase beyond its function—something to sit on.

When he adds that it is a brown, leather easy chair he is providing a few more generalizations. The word, *brown,* covers all objects of this color. The word, *leather,* includes all things made of this substance. And the word, *easy,* embraces all chairs in which one can sink fairly deeply. In effect, he is closing in on the idea by adding successive generalizations that the object must fit. We talk then in generalizations. And when we want to become more specific we just add a few more generalizations.

Thinking, on the other hand, starts with specifics. When we think, most of us form pictures in our mind. And pictures represent a particular object or event.

One can't think of chairs in general. One has to form a mental picture of a specific chair and let it stand for the general idea of chair. For you can't make a picture of a generalization. And different people form different images for the idea of *chair,* as well as for any other word.

The tendency to think in images is illustrated by our use of metaphors to facilitate communication. For example, the words: courage, fragrance and purity are conveyed more effectively when associating them with mental pictures: the courage of a lion; the fragrance of a flower; and the purity of freshly fallen snow.

Words Convey Only Parts Of Mental Images

Since we think in images we can't convey our thoughts in their entirety. For we can't capture a total image through the use of words. All we can do is keep adding words to describe further parts or aspects, of which there are almost an infinite number.

For example, we can't put into words the totality of another person. We can only talk about aspects of him: his ability, his clothes, his honesty, his sexual prowess, his fatherhood or any of thousands of other aspects. Similarly, suppose you are walking through a forest and want to put your impressions into words. You can't convey the whole thing. Words can only carry one aspect at a time. The aspects you choose to convey will very likely be related to your particular interests. You might talk about trees or earth or bird sounds or smells or shadows or any of a myriad of other aspects.

Even when we seem to be talking about a totality, e.g., "I like him," we are still only referring to a particular aspect. In this case it isn't the totality of "him" that's being discussed, but the *speaker's fondness* for "him."

Let's consider then what happens in conversation. One person has an image in mind. He puts into words a particular aspect of that image. The other person, hearing the words, builds his own image, on the basis of the aspect communicated. The total image in one person's mind will not be the same as that in the other person's mind, since only a particular aspect is communicated. All the rest of the image formed depends on interests, wishes, and past experiences; and these, of course, will be different for different individuals.

This divergence in total images doesn't matter as long as the particular aspect in common is the only item of concern. For example, if someone asks you if a particular person is tall, and you answer yes, he may visualize a tall, broad man while you have an image of a tall, slim one. But this discrepancy in images doesn't distort communication since height is the only point of concern.

Similarly, if one person says to another, "I think it's a good thing for a boy to have a dog," it doesn't really matter if one person visualizes a large, shaggy sheep dog while the other imagines a smooth, little terrier. The concept of boy-having-dog is the only aspect that's pertinent, and this can be discussed apart from the topic of breeds.

However, differences in mental images do produce a good deal of misunderstanding. This happens when people do not put into words all the aspects that are pertinent. A common illusion is responsible for this. People often don't realize that words can only communicate aspects. They think instead that words represent total images. When they talk about their mental images they assume that the whole image, instead of just an aspect, is being transferred. They therefore think that the other person has greater understanding of their thinking than he really does.

The following conversation illustrates how communicating too few aspects results in misunderstanding.

"I'm getting a big bang out of a new book I'm reading."

"Yeah, I like books with a lot of humor in them."

"Well, this isn't a humorous book. It's got a lot of action in it, though."

"Action, eh? That's what I like, a good book about sports."

"This isn't about sports. It's a story about Africa."

"Oh, I know what you mean. Big game hunting, safaris. I haven't read a book like that in a long time now.

"No, no, it isn't that kind of thing at all. It's about politics."

"Oh, you mean that kind of action. Yeah, politics is a fast game today. All that intrigue in Washington. Atomic energy, the U.N., and everybody fighting to get his share Must be a lively book, all right."

"No, this takes place in the Congo. It shows all the political maneuvering. What goes on when the leaders fight for control of a new country."

As an extension of this, when two people in conversation do not identify the particular aspect they are discussing and think instead that they are talking about total images, each is talking about something different from the other. For the total images are never the same.

Let's take an example. One person asks another, "Do you

think I should ask my father for his advice on this matter?" The second person doesn't know the father; and when the word, father, is mentioned the image of a harsh, egocentric dictator comes to his mind because of his own experience. The first person, on the other hand, actually has a kindly, helpful father.

The second person frames a reply on the basis of his image of his own father. He is not aware that this is prompting his recommendation. He says, "I think you ought to stand on your own two feet, make your own decisions." Now, this statement as a generalization has the sound of good sense. However, it might not at all apply in this specific situation and it might very well be motivated by the second person's anger at his father. It would be more appropriate for the second person to answer, "That depends on your relationship with your father. What's he like?"

In this case the trouble was caused by each thinking that since they both used the same word, father, they both had the same mental image. And this misconception stems from the false notion that the word, father, stands for the total image of father when all it signifies is one aspect—the paternal role.

Feed Back To Separate
Observation From Interpretation

When we form a mental image of something we have observed we often add to this image things we associate with it. Then the line blurs between what we observed and what we added and it seems to us that we actually observed the whole of our mental image.

In reporting his observations to you the other person will often be fusing his interpretation with what he actually saw. Since his interpretation is included as direct observation you will tend to accept it as fact. Yet you will be misinformed about what happened whenever his interpretation is wrong.

To separate the other person's observations from his interpretations, visualize in your mind what he is describing and feed back other details of the scene as it appears in your mental image. These are events that would seem to you to have occurred if his report truly represents what he saw.

As you feed back these filled-in details and he verifies whether or not he observed them, his interpretations will stand out as separate from his observations. An example of this separating of observation from interpretation is the following cross-examination of a witness in court.

> LAWYER: Would you please describe exactly what you saw?
>
> WITNESS: Well, I was walking down Elm Street on my way home—actually I was almost running because I was in a terrible hurry—and as I came near Mr. Jenkin's house—I was on the other side of the street—I saw Mr. Jenkins stretched out on the sidewalk and the defendant hitting him with his cane. I didn't think I would be able to stop him—I'm not very athletic—so I ran ahead to my home, which is on the corner of the same street, and called the police.
>
> LAWYER: Think carefully now. Did you actually see the cane come in contact with Mr. Jenkins' body?
>
> WITNESS: Let's see now. No, I can't say I did. You see I was in a big hurry. I didn't wait around to watch it.
>
> LAWYER: Then it's possible that the cane never did actually strike Mr. Jenkins.
>
> WITNESS: Well, I don't see what else the defendant was doing. He was bending over Mr. Jenkins and the cane was raised above his head ready to strike.
>
> LAWYER: Isn't it possible that the defendent found Mr. Jenkins lying there, was bending over to examine him and was holding the cane above his head to get it out of the way so that he could comfortably bend over?

The closer you stay to words that describe what you actually saw or heard the less likely you are to communicate false information. Certainly you should interpret situations. But try to give along with your interpretations as much of your actual observations as possible, so that the other person has a chance to test the plausibility of other possible interpretations.

A sales executive described to me a sales applicant that he had just interviewed as being imaginative. When I asked him why he considered the applicant imaginative, he replied that as part of the interview he had asked the applicant to sell him a pencil.

The applicant presented his pencil as having the following benefits: the lead is unbreakable; the eraser doesn't wear down at all; and erasures aren't noticeable. The executive felt that it was very imaginative of the sales applicant to think of these benefits and that he certainly would have sold the pencil.

I asked the executive if there is any such pencil on the market or if it is presently feasible. When he admitted he didn't know of any, I suggested that the applicant was taking the easy way and that the benefits represented wishful thinking rather than a constructive use of imagination. I left him with the question, How good a salesman will he be if he has to rely on product features that are so good they don't even exist?

The sales executive used the word, *imaginative*, to denote a ready flow of ideas without regard to the practicality of these ideas. Then, in using this word to describe the applicant the sales executive might develop in the mind of a listener an image of a person who uses a prolific imagination constructively. Unless the listener checked with the sales executive to find out what he meant by imaginative, they would have a different impression of the same individual.

As the Conversation Proceeds Compare Your Mental Image With The Other Person's

Two people in conversation are never talking about exactly the same thing. As the conversation progresses the succession of images in one mind is never quite the same as that in the other. Remember that when one forms an image he can only put in words a part of that image. The other person, hearing that part, reconstructs his own total image from the part communicated.

Each person's total image might be quite different from the other's, depending on the words used and how they are interpreted. But no matter how full and precise the words are, there will still be some dissimilarity between the images since the two people have different past experiences, different emotional reactions, and different attitudes and wishes.

Let's take an example. Suppose John is telling Mary about an airplane trip he has taken. Mary has never travelled by plane. Let's listen to a part of the conversation and compare mental images.

> JOHN: The food is very good. It's so tasty and there's quite a variety.
>
> (In John's mental image there is a tray on his lap and on the tray are a steak, mashed potatoes and string beans, along with other courses and utensils that formed his last meal on a plane. Mary's mental image contains a table with a linen tablecloth and regular place settings. And she sees a fancy piece of French pastry.)
>
> MARY: Sounds wonderful. What is the service like?
>
> (As Mary asks this she sees in her mind black-suited waiters scurrying around.)
>
> JOHN: Oh, the food is served by very pretty and friendly stewardesses. They're always ready to help you in any way that they can.
>
> (John recalls an image of a stewardess that he particularly liked. She is of medium height with dark hair and big brown eyes. She has a square face, a slightly plumpish figure, and smiles very readily. Mary imagines at the same time a tall, blond, slim young girl with an oval face, wearing a bright, shiny dress.)
>
> MARY: Is it noisy in the plane?
>
> JOHN: A little. It depends pretty much on where you sit.

(Mary immediately thinks of a high-pitched clattering noise while John is recalling a low-pitched, humming sound.)

Even when they are talking about very specific things such as food and stewardesses and noise, the images are quite different. If at this point Mary were to say to John that she would be afraid to fly, her image of disaster would be different from his.

If Mary were to plan to travel by plane in the near future she would probably expect the same delicious pastry she brought to mind in this conversation and would look for a tall, blond stewardess with an oval face. She might even make inquiries beforehand as to where she should sit to avoid the high-pitched, clattering noise.

In order to make sure that they are talking about the same thing two people in conversation should exchange images every so often. It is somewhat like a ship's captain periodically check-ing his bearings to make sure that he is on course.

Feed Back Your Interpretation Rather Than The Other Person's Words

In conversation the checking of images is done by *feeding back*. This means that at intervals in a conversation each person describes to the other the relevant aspects of the image in his mind just to make sure that they are both talking about the same thing. The other person can then indicate whether or not this corresponds to his image. When you are doing the talking, if the other person doesn't feed back, it would be wise for you to ask him to do so.

In feeding back it is especially important not to use the same words that the other person has used. If you do, and he agrees that this is what he said, you only know that you heard his words correctly but not that your image is what he *meant*. Therefore, rather than saying back his words you should describe to him in your own words the relevant parts of your image. An effective variation on describing back to him your impression of what he meant is to give back to him your expectation of the consequences of what he seems to be saying. If these consequences are not what he expects, the reason may lie in your misunderstanding of what he meant.

Let's take an example. Suppose a doctor has just finished taping a patient's foot because of a sprained ligament. The conversation continues as follows:

DOCTOR: There, I think that will make you feel better. Keep the tape on till Wednesday and call me.

(The patient could interpret the doctor's statement to mean that the tape should be removed on Wednesday and that the patient should call the doctor to let him know how it feels. Or the doctor's remark could be interpreted as indicating that the patient should call the doctor on Wednesday to see what should be done. The doctor might have meant one thing and the patient might have interpreted it as another, and each might see his image so clearly that he assumes that this is what the other person means. Let's see what happens, however, if the patient feeds back his own image to the doctor.)

PATIENT: You want me to take off the tape Wednesday evening, I suppose, and then call you. Is that right?

(Note that the feedback here is also designed to find out whether the doctor meant morning or evening as well as whether he meant for the tape to come off Wednesday at all.)

DOCTOR: Oh no. You will probably have to keep the tape on until Friday. Call me Wednesday just to let me know how it feels.

In the above example the patient's describing explicitly what he intended to do, based on his interpretation of the doctor's instructions, brought out the discrepancy.

Let's take a case where the listener feeds back by describing the consequences he expects based on his interpretation of what the other person is saying. In this case an executive is talking with a subordinate.

EXECUTIVE: This project is very important. Better give it your full attention.

(This could be interpreted by the subordinate as meaning, put everything else aside until this project is completed. Or the executive could have meant, be particularly thorough in handling this job.)

SUBORDINATE: I guess you want me to drop everything else, then.

(Here the subordinate feeds back the consequences, based on his interpretation rather than actually describing the interpretation, itself.)

EXECUTIVE: Let's see now. You're also working on the *Consolidated* project.

SUBORDINATE: Yes, and it's taking a good bit of my time.

EXECUTIVE: Well, that's too important to let ride. Maybe we'd better get you some help so you can carry on with both these projects.

If the subordinate had not fed back his interpretation he might very well have dropped the *Consolidated* project. As a result, the expected progress on it would not have occurred, resulting in possible loss to the company and an angry boss.

Keep in mind that unless you check with the other person you really have no way of knowing for sure whether or not you understand correctly what he means. It isn't as though in one case you will develop an image and in the other case you won't. You will always develop an image from your own associations, and the very existence of an image in your mind leads you to believe that you know what the other person has in mind.

Since you can't be sure you have understood correctly merely by examining your own image it is safer to periodically feed back during the conversation *whether or not you think you understand what is meant.*

In addition to clarifying, feeding back can serve two other purposes : (1) helping another person gain insight; and (2) influencing him.

Feeding Back To Give Insight

Another person's image may not be clear in his own mind. He may not be sure of what he means. From his words you might construct a unified image in your mind which you then give back to him. This can suddenly crystallize in his mind a new realization.

The conversation below provides an example of how feedback is used to help another person gain self-insight. Here, a teacher is talking to one of his students.

TEACHER: Mary, I notice you never try to participate when we have class discussions.

MARY: I don't really have anything to add to what the others say.

TEACHER: From the quizzes, you seem to know the material well.

MARY: That's different.

TEACHER: Different?

MARY: I have time to think during the quizzes so that I don't make mistakes. But when you ask a question for discussion somebody else is always ready to answer it before I have time to think about it.

TEACHER: You mean when I ask the class a question other students think of the answer faster than you do?

(At this point the teacher is feeding back to make sure he understands what she means.)

MARY: Well, I often know the answer right off but I like to think about it some more to make sure it's not wrong.

TEACHER: After you think about it do you generally find it's wrong?

MARY: No, not really.

TEACHER: Well, then, if thinking about it doesn't change your answer anyway you must be thinking about it for some other reason. Maybe you're frightened of making a mistake. You might feel that it's a terrible thing to be wrong.

(The teacher feeds back to help Mary gain self-insight.)
MARY: (pauses) Yes, I guess I do feel that way.

In the above conversation the teacher confronts Mary with an idea which had never quite formed in her mind. She never realized how afraid she was of being wrong, or perhaps she didn't want to face it. When this idea is formed in front of her from the things she has said, and then fed back she recognizes it to be true.

Feeding Back To Influence

Often in a discussion a person will make an invalid statement that on the face of it seems to make sense. At least it does to him. However, when faced with its implications he comes to realize that it is untenable, and is likely to lead to trouble. As a result of feeding back to him the undesirable results of his position he is motivated to take a new one.

Let's watch a salesman dislodge a buyer from a position of resistance.

SALESMAN: I've got a new model that is really going to make money for you.
BUYER: I'm not interested in seeing anything new.
SALESMAN: How come?
BUYER: I've got too much stock as it is. I can't afford to buy anymore until I move what I have.
SALESMAN: We're putting on a big pre-tested promotion on this model with heavy national advertising in all the magazines. And we have a really good deal on local advertising. You'll get plenty of calls for it.
BUYER: I'll wait until I get the calls before I order it.
SALESMAN: Then you're willing to lose a lot of sales and send a lot of your customers to your competitors during the two weeks it takes to get delivery.
(Here the salesman feeds back an undesirable image resulting from the position the buyer has taken.)
BUYER: I don't like to lose any sales but I simply can't afford to tie up any more money in inventory.

SALESMAN: I appreciate your reluctance to increase your stock but why not get rid of your slow-moving merchandise by marking it down? Run a sale.

BUYER: Run a sale? I'm not in business just to move merchandise. I want to make some money.

SALESMAN: And you feel that stock sitting on your shelves is going to make more money than merchandise that really moves on the wave of a big promotion.

(The salesman again feeds back an undesirable image resulting from the buyer's position.)

BUYER: All right. What's the deal?

The buyer's thinking is influenced by feeding back to him an image that logically follows from what he has said, and yet is unacceptable to him. To change this image he has to change his position.

Keep These Ideas In Mind

Words represent only aspects of images and can never convey total images. Therefore, you're never talking about total images but only about aspects. Be sure to identify which aspects are being discussed.

The same words produce different mental images in different people.

Feed back your interpretation of what's being said and get the other person to do the same.

7

Holding People's Attention

Don't Take More Time Than A Subject Is Worth

People can concentrate on only one thing at a time. And at any given moment there are many things competing for this concentration. In conversation, you have to hold the narrow, unstable beam of the other person's attention focused on what you say, for this is your only point of contact with his mind. As soon as the beam wavers you are merely talking to yourself.

How do you keep him focused on your talk? It's really a matter of economy. The waiting room for his attention is always crowded. He has so many things he wants to think about. Since his attention is limited he will be motivated to give it where he feels he will get the most return. Your listener's attention will be held when what you have to say is useful, easy to grasp and worth the time it takes to tell it. Let's see how we make it so.

Stick To The Point

Talking to the point means communicating only those ideas which contribute to the idea-pattern you're trying to convey. As you feed ideas to your listener he tries to fit them together to form a pattern. Leave out ideas that don't belong to this pattern.

From your introductory remarks the other person gets a general idea of where you are heading. He expects each subsequent remark to have a bearing on the discussion-objective. At the same time, he puts a value on this objective in terms of the time it's worth. When the discussion exceeds this time he begins to lose interest and his attention wanders.

Any comment that does not contribute to the other person's understanding of the discussion-objective is beside the point. Though it may serve some purpose for you, and therefore, have relevancy to this purpose, it is irrelevant for him.

Irrelevancy Is Caused By Personality Needs

People don't wander accidentally into irrelevancy. Something other than the discussion-objective is more relevant for them at the moment, although it may be far afield. They have a need to express something which is greater than their wish to stick to the point. They may want to impress others, get more attention, find a sounding-board for their own ideas or satisfy their curiosity about the other person's feelings.

In the example below we find all of these entering, and pulling the conversation away from the objective. Here, a subordinate is reporting to his supervisor.

SUPERVISOR: Did you get the information?

SUBORDINATE: Well, I called on the people you asked me to. Some of them were very nice and cooperative. I enjoyed talking to them. Others were difficult. Didn't want to say anything. It took a lot of tact and persistence to get the information.

SUPERVISOR: It wasn't an easy job but I felt you could handle it.

SUBORDINATE: Oh, I didn't really have any trouble. There was one fellow who must have been lonely. He kept talking about all kinds of things. It took a lot of patience to get the information out of him.

SUPERVISOR: Well, I'm glad you got it. I think it will be very useful. When do you think you'll have the report on it ready?

SUBORDINATE: It's going to take a while to get the material organized. I want to do a careful job of extracting the significant ideas and backing them up by actual quotes. I thought also that you might want me to have some more interviews. I mean do you think the sample is large enough?

SUPERVISOR: Yes, of course. We've done this kind of study before.

SUBORDINATE: Oh, you have. What did you find out? I mean was it for the same kind of operation?

SUPERVISOR: Yes, very similar. I can't go into it now but you can find the material in the files. Do you think you could have the report by the end of next week?

SUBORDINATE: The end of next week? I think so. I had some ideas on how I might organize the report that I wanted to explore with you.

In the above example, the subordinate's need to point up his tact, persistence, patience and care caused the introduction of irrelevant material. Later in the discussion the need for more attention, the wish for a sounding board, and curiosity probably all played a role.

From the supervisor's point of view all that was relevant was that the information had been gotten, and that the report would be ready by the end of next week.

Irrelevancy results from the fact that people need to talk to others in order to let out their feelings and establish human contact, and not just for the transmission of information. People need to feel in touch with each other. They want to be reminded that others care about them. They want to express themselves, and often they'd like the approval of others. Without fulfillment of these needs many people experience a sense of isolation.

One then turns to conversation as a way of fulfillment. But there's the counter force of embarrassment at using up other people's time to satisfy these personality needs. So a compromise is made. Pursuit of these satisfactions is worked into discussions ostensibly aimed at logical goals. The result is a wavy rather than a straight-line conversational course toward the discussion objective.

Irrelevancy is an expression of the individual seeking satisfaction of personality needs. He is often not aware of his own irrelevancy simply because the irrelevancy implies the presence of personality pressures which the individual may not want to face. He might not admit to himself that he needs approval or that he wants attention simply to feel cared about. And it could be difficult for him to accept his not having sufficient control to prevent his needs from intruding on his purposeful conversation.

The individual who is addicted to digressions is as much a victim as are his listeners. They may writhe impatiently as they attempt to follow his meanderings, never getting within grasp of the point of the conversation; but he is unable to help himself. He is being driven by the discomfort of his personality weaknesses to move in any direction that promises amelioration.

There are so many things one wants to say that are really of little interest to other people. One wants to display intellect, give evidence of virtue, prove one's skill, influence others and discharge emotions. But who will listen attentively to all this? So what else can one do but work these expressions into the fabric of businesslike conversation where others are attentive because of their own interests?

Listening to the other person's irrelevancy can enrich your understanding of him. You can glimpse his personality needs and can even help him satisfy them through your sympathetic response. But what about your own irrelevancy? You may not want to impose on the other person's tolerance.

In order to head straight for your discussion-objective you have to keep it always in sight. Ask yourself as you talk, What has this to do with the point in question? Would I want to listen to it?

Don't fall into the trap of deciding that something is relevant because it is *interesting*. Choosing so vague a criterion as *interesting* in order to decide whether to introduce an idea will be giving yourself license to push all kinds of clutter into your talk. It's easy to rationalize that something is interesting if one wants to say it badly enough.

Another question to ask yourself is, Does this idea contribute to understanding of the point, or am I trying to bring it in for some other purpose? If your answer indicates that this new idea is for some personal purpose rather than being related to the main point, this does not necessarily mean that you shouldn't express it. But if you're going to be irrelevant you ought at least know what you're doing and keep it under control.

Keep Your Speeches Short

Attention continually drifts away and back to the subject at hand. It does not focus steadily on anything. The best one can hope for in a listener is that his attention keep coming back. Therefore, when feeding him ideas you should only give him one at a time. Even while he is focusing on your words he has to digest one idea before he can take in the next.

Too many sales are lost simply because salesmen talk too much. Similarly, executives, in an effort to save time, too often crowd all their messages into one speech. Actually they're wasting time since they will have to go over the same material again because most of it is never caught by the listener.

If you are trying to educate or influence others you oughtn't to speak for more than about 20 seconds at any one time. Your listener can't absorb any more than this in one bite. In order to absorb material he has to think about it; and he can't be thinking about an idea you've just fed him and be listening to your next one at the same time.

To demonstrate why speeches should be short let's listen for a moment to a salesman talking to a buyer.

> "Mr. Brown, let me show you why my product is such a terrific buy that it's in demand all over the country. This is the hottest number we've had in years. Look at the design—the smooth, modern clean lines. This was designed by one of the best men in the country. He's won all kinds of prizes. And this product was built to last. It's really durable. It can take all kinds of knocking around. It's got a one-year guarantee, anyway, but it's built to last a life time. And this product is number one in our advertising. It's all over the place—radio, TV, the big magazines, with a terrific deal for you on local advertising. And for a quality item like this the price is very, very low, with good terms and with especially good discounts for volume buying and with fast delivery also, which is gonna really be needed because this stuff is gonna really move off your shelves."

Suppose you look away from this book for a moment and see how many of the salesman's arguments you've absorbed. And how does a salesman sell a buyer who doesn't absorb the arguments?

The salesman should have presented one idea at a time in short speeches, and then asked the buyer what he thinks of it. For example, after pointing out the attractiveness of the design he could have elicited the buyer's reactions. Similarly, after each of the subsequent benefits—construction, advertising, and price—the salesman should have encouraged comment. Getting the buyer to comment on an idea is a way of making him absorb it, since he must absorb before he can comment.

In addition to getting frequent feed-back from the listener, you ought to space the significant ideas. He can't build his mental image as fast as you can throw image parts at him. For this reason key words, particularly adjectives, generally carry too much meaning for communicating in a series. For example, if the salesman above had merely said, "This product is attractive, durable, well-advertised, and economical," his speech would have been quite short; but at the same time it would have been too compressed to be readily grasped. Four adjectives in a row are too many to take in unless the person memorizes them and then works them over in his mind. The trouble is that the speaker has generally gone on to some other topic while the listener is still fumbling with what he heard.

Two adjectives at a time are plenty. If someone describes a man as tall and thin you get an immediate picture. But if someone says that a man is tall, stocky, paunchy, and nearsighted, you have to stop for a moment and put these adjectives together in their proper places. Even three adjectives in a row, e.g., round, heavy and shiny, make you pause for a moment to integrate them, to form the corresponding mental image.

If you have four adjectives to convey, give them two at a time and ask for comment in between. Or else, give the adjectives more space by elaborating a bit on each. For example, in describing the second man, above, you might say something like, "He was tall and stood up straight so that his height looked still more impressive. He barely managed to keep his too-tight jacket buttoned, perhaps in a vain attempt to hide an aggressive paunch. He was bald except for a few strands of light brown hair which he combed straight back, and for side-burns which were speckled with gray. And he wore horn-rimmed glasses low on his stub nose."

Of course, more information is provided here. However, more time isn't necessarily used since if the four adjectives are fed one after another, time would have to be allowed for them to sink in. And this time might just as well be used by filling out the picture.

Obviousness Causes Tuning Out

While you should allow enough time between ideas so that your listener can absorb them, too much time will result in losing his attention. Excessive time is often unwittingly provided by repetitiveness and by saying things that are obvious to him. These do not keep his mind active. The conversational *pace* becomes too slow.

Watch the pacing of ideas in your conversation. Pacing can make the difference between stimulating and dull discussion. If your ideas are presented at a brisk pace your listener tries to maintain attention in order to keep up. This mental activity stimulates him. He finds his mind refreshed by new ideas.

Saying the obvious not only bores the listener but carries with it the implicit message that you think he is either ignorant or stupid. And if you repeat your words you imply that his powers of hearing or comprehension are inadequate. He is not only likely to become annoyed but will probably tune out, preferring to give his attention to inner concerns or other events around him, where there is more gain.

Although obviousness is deadening to a conversation it abounds in everyday discussions. The abundance of obviousness and repetitiveness is further evidence that conversation serves purposes other than the transmitting of information. Here, personality needs—to discharge feeling, to be in touch with another mind, and to allay anxiety about the listener's not comprehending—exert enough pressure to make one risk being boring, by telling another person what he already knows.

Consider, for example, how little information is exchanged in the following conversation:

> "The trouble nowadays is that kids have no respect for their parents, and parents let them get away with it."
> "Yeah, that's right. The kids push their parents around. There's no discipline."

"Parents used to lay down the law, and the kids used to do what they were told."

"That's right. You didn't find the kids running wild, doing anything they pleased, the way they do today."

"You're darn right they didn't run wild. Because if they did they'd really have it coming, and they'd get it too."

"People seem to be too afraid of saying the wrong things to their kids like they were going to deform their personalities or something. Seems to me like you got to form them before you can deform them."

"That's right. People aren't raising their kids anymore. The kids are raising themselves."

"Yeah. It's the kids who run the home."

If the motive for the above conversation were merely a rational exchange of information the whole thing could have been accomplished by one person saying: "Children seem to be running wild these days and parents seem to be afraid to exert any discipline"; and the other person could reply, "Yes, I quite agree."

Bring In Fresh Information

Going over and over the same material causes the conversation to wear thin. While cordiality might be promoted since each is sympathetic to the other's viewpoint, interest is likely to wane. Thinking stops and the conversation lapses into a kind of mechanical hum as each discharges his feelings. When the emotional pressures have been released the conversation no longer serves any purpose, and the rut becomes stifling. This is followed by a movement toward separation and each goes his way.

Of course, you may ask, But why must one work at every conversation? Why can't one just talk easily about whatever comes to mind rather than trying to be stimulating? After all everyone has feelings to discharge.

Certainly everyone has feelings to discharge; but why not

discharge them in a stimulating manner, having the pleasure of active mental play, and making the other person glad to be involved.

A sound way of stimulating interest is bringing new information into the conversation. Giving your listener new facts and fresh insights is bound to hold his attention. Starting him thinking about things he hadn't considered before makes the discussion an adventure for him.

For example, suppose the participants in the above conversation had done the following: told about specific incidents in their childhood when discipline had been enforced; explored why parents seem afraid of their children; raised questions about what happens to a child's personality when there is too little or too much discipline; and exchanged how each other's spouses feel about the matter.

All this requires more mental effort. One must search one's memory, formulate pertinent questions, and find sensible answers. But the result is quite rewarding. Not only does it mean enriched conversation that holds attention but it makes for more alert, aggressive thinking.

When Repeating Give More Information

Repetition is often useful. The more often a person hears something the more likely he is to retain it. Furthermore, since his attention drifts in and out he may catch something the second time that he missed the first. The problem is to hold his attention while repeating. For he is likely to tune out on the mere repetition of words he has heard before.

In order to hold his interest you have to give something additional with each repetition. Don't repeat the same words. Instead, give him a larger view of the same thing. When you do this you are still including what you presented before, and therefore accomplishing a repetition, but without boring your listener.

For example, when you give an instruction follow this with the reason. Explaining why adds something new but at the same time it contains within it a repetition of the instruction. All the time that you are explaining why, the instruction itself is before his mind.

Another alternative is to suggest a likely outcome. Again, discussion of the outcome holds the original instruction in his mind. Some other worthwhile ways of repeating are: talking about the background; describing similar situations; and presenting alternatives.

As an illustration, if a doctor instructs a patient to take a particular pill three times a day and then elaborates on this by saying, one after each meal, this elaboration is a way of repeating the idea of three times.

As a further example, suppose a teacher were giving the following assignment to his class: "Read chapter 2 in your text and then prepare five questions that you would ask if you were giving a quiz on the chapter. Preparing quiz questions requires you to think about the material." Giving the reason for assigning the preparation of quiz questions was a way of repeating the assignment in an interesting manner.

Use Concrete Words

One way of classifying words is by how readily they evoke corresponding mental images. For example, the words: lamp, knife, dancing, dog, and eating stimulate specific mental images. But how does one develop a mental picture for such words as: freedom, honesty, charity, integrity, or justice?

Words that stand for objects (lamp, dog, etc.), or for activities (dancing, eating, etc.) which one can visualize, are *concrete* words. Words that stand for ideas that cannot be visualized (honesty, goodness, etc.) are *abstract* words. An abstract word can be applied in such a great variety of ways that no single way would truly convey its meaning. And since only one way at a time can be visualized, abstract words cannot be pictured in one's mind. Of course concreteness and abstractness are not absolutes. There are varying degrees of each. Words are on a continuum between these opposite poles, and a word is called one or the other when it tends more toward that pole.

As an example of the difficulty of visualizing an abstract word suppose that you say about a man that he is *kind*. You cannot form a picture of kindness. You can only imagine a particular kindly act. For example, you might think of this man visiting a sick friend. But kindness means much more than this. It includes the multitude of various kindly acts that this man performs on a day-to-day basis. He may be: hospitable to visitors; considerate of the needs of subordinates; and generous with his possessions. And here again we become involved with abstract words: hospitable, considerate, and generous.

Since each abstract word covers a wide variety of possible images, and since we think in specific images, it is quite likely that the person using an abstract word has a very different image in mind from that of his listener. Abstract words embrace so much that their use frequently results in: heated argument between two people who are basically in agreement; apparent agreement when both have very different things in mind; and even self-deception.

But abstract words are not just villains causing muddled communication. They represent a higher order of intellectual activity than do concrete words, and make possible more complex problem-solving. Abstract words designate aspects shared by many more different kinds of objects or events than do aspects denoted by concrete words. For example, the abstract word, *good* can be used in a much greater variety of ways than can the concrete word, *painted*.

Abstract words are necessary and useful for involved thinking. But they cover such large areas over which the mind can range that they must be defined whenever used in order for minds to meet. Never let them stand by themselves. Only concrete words can stand alone. When using abstract words always make sure that you follow their use with an example or explanation in concrete words so that images in the other person's mind conform to the way you mean the abstract words.

Practice These Methods For Holding Attention

Here are the essential ideas to keep in mind for holding your listener's attention:

1. Stick to the point.

2. Space your ideas by keeping your speeches short. This gives your listener time to think about each idea as it is presented.

3. Don't tell the other person what he already knows. Repeat your meaning but not your words, and avoid saying the obvious.

4. Use concrete words whenever possible. Whenever you use abstract words illustrate them through the use of concrete ones.

Practice applying these methods in your next conversation. Note when your attention is held and when it seems to drift away. Try to analyze why this happens and how the use of these methods affects it.

8

Activating Thinking

There Are No Right Words

One common illusion about conversation is that the *right* words will plant ideas firmly in the mind of the listener. It's as though certain magic phrases are the key to getting through. The result of this illusion is that many people arrange and re-arrange their words, try varying degrees of forcefulness in their tone, spice their sentences with wit and then wonder why the listener isn't won over by such a brilliant array of logic, imaginativeness, vitality, and humor.

They assume that because the listener is silent he is absorbing the messages. He is adressed as though he were a recording machine, taking down everything that's spoken.

Actually, there are no right words. For it doesn't matter much which words are used. as long as your meaning is clear. What really determines whether your message gets into the mind of the listener is his level of listening, that is his mental activity.

The Three Levels Of Listening

Your conversational partner may participate on any of three levels of mental activity.

1. THE NON-HEARING LEVEL. First, there is the level where he's not listening at all. He may gaze raptly into your eyes, nod periodically, and even utter such deceptive indicators of attention as, "I see," "Mm," "You've got a point there."

2. THE LEVEL OF HEARING. Second, there is the level of listening where he remembers the words you are saying. If you were to stop suddenly and ask him what you just said he would be able to repeat back the last sentence or two. However, there is no real absorption of ideas; as soon as the conversation ends, your ideas have evaporated from the surface of his mind.

3. THE LEVEL OF THINKING. Third, there is the level where your listener *thinks* about what you are saying. Thinking about something means doing mental work on it—evaluating it, comparing it with something else, analyzing for its causes, predicting likely outcomes, or making a decision about it. In order for you to be getting your ideas into the mind of your listener he has to be listening to them on this level. Anything less than this is merely an alternating of talking rather than an interchange of ideas.

Keep in mind that the other person has different experiences from you, different values, a different frame of reference, a different way of looking at things, and is even likely to use different words to say the same thing. In order to grasp your ideas he has to fit them into his scheme of thinking. It isn't just a matter of hearing what you say. He has to visualize your ideas in the way he would use them.

Your ideas will not be absorbed by him if he merely considers them in the abstract. He has to imagine these ideas in operation in some situation that involves him. He has to transform your ideas, shape them to fit his life-pattern.

Your Listener Won't Want To Bother Thinking

Thinking purposefully is work. To solve problems the mind must be harnessed. It must follow the rules of logic and be limited by what is realistically possible.

It is often so much more pleasant to drift mentally, to dream about goals achieved and rewards gained, to fantasy revenge, or even to suffer a tragic fate, perhaps as heroic victim, in the theatre of the mind. And your listener is likely to feel that if he isn't going to indulge in this mental free play, he might just as well think about his own problems rather than yours.

Your listener is not likely on his own initiative to listen at the thinking level. He would prefer while you are talking to let his mind idle or to think his own thoughts. If he is going to go so far as to listen to what you are saying rather than drifting away while you talk, he will probably just sit back and passively let your words glide over the surface of his mind, and reserve his mental energy for his personal interests.

After Presenting Ideas You Have To Stimulate The Other Person To Think

When you are trying to influence someone's thinking your responsibility does not end with putting your ideas into words. You can't just say to yourself, Well I've done my share in putting my thoughts in clear, well-organized, sensible terms. It's up to him to grasp it. If your communicating goes only as far as verbalizing your ideas, you'll not be getting through.

You have to go beyond saying what's on your mind, no matter how well you put it. You need to reach out and make his mind work on it. This is part of your conversational responsibility. If you're selling something, you haven't really done your job if you stop at telling about your product, no matter how well you tell it. Even asking for an order is not in itself enough. You have to make his mind evaluate every one of the benefits you offer him. Unless you do this you are not likely to have a meeting of minds but just an exchange of words.

Stimulate Thinking By Asking Questions

How do you make the other person think about your ideas? The answer is, by asking him a question.

In Chapter three, techniques of questioning were given for drawing out information. In contrast, the purpose of questioning as described in this chapter, is to stimulate the other person to think about your ideas, since this is necessary in order for him to grasp them. Here, questioning is used not to uncover his thoughts but to implant yours.

The question is a remarkable conversational instrument. When used skillfully it can point the way to the solution of a problem. It can give an individual insight into his own feelings and motivations or into those of another person. It can arouse a mind from its inertia and set it into motion.

Success in scientific research depends very much on whether one puts the right questions to nature. The scientific experiment is an attempt to answer a question. But often, thinking of the crucial question to ask is the really creative part of the experiment, and the key to one of nature's secrets.

Since a question is a request for information, in order to supply it the other person has to move from the passive, listening state to the active, thinking one. He has to reach in his mind for the answer or perhaps work it out. Then he has to put it into language in order to communicate it. If the question you ask him is related to something you just told him, you are making his mind work on your ideas.

Keep in mind that the telling of something is only the first step in getting it across. In order to absorb your ideas the listener has to mentally react to them; and you have to ask him to react. Let's take an example.

A supervisor is giving a subordinate some constructive criticism:

"Tom, I want to talk to you about your reports. I'm not very happy with them. They don't really give me a clear picture of what's happening. I read them and I'm left all at sea because they raise so many unanswered questions in my mind. What you do in your reports is give me your interpretation; but you don't tell me what you base your interpretation on. For example, you say in a report that the morale of the men in your section is low. What do you base this on? Are there more complaints? Are they quitting the job? You say the new machines aren't performing as well as the old ones did. What do you mean by not performing as well? Are there more breakdowns? Are they turning out less work? Are they harder to operate? I'd like to know the evidence on which you base your judgments. See that you provide it in future reports."

The subordinate might or might not absorb the superior's request depending on how alert the subordinate is. Or he might not agree. He might resent the criticism—or his interpretation of it—and refuse to think about it. At the same time he might not say anything, merely nodding and walking away. How much surer would the superior have been of his request being grasped and accepted if the conversation had gone like this:

"Tom, I read your reports carefully since I am most concerned about what is going on in your section but too often I'm not sure of what you mean. You give me your opinion about the conditions in your section but you don't give me the evidence to back it up. Are you aware that you're doing this?"

(The supervisor ends with a question to get a reaction.)

"If you mean that I don't give you all the details in a report, well I didn't think you'd want them. I try to give you straight, to-the-point reports. I know you've got a lot of stuff to read."

(Subordinate either doesn't grasp or doesn't accept supervisor's point.)

"I appreciate your trying to boil down your reports to the essentials, but I still need the evidence on which you base your opinions. For example, in a recent report you mentioned that the morale of the men in your section is low. Well, unless you tell me what you base this on, whether it's high worker turnover, too many complaints, absenteeism, etc., I don't exactly know what you mean by low morale. Is it a real crisis or is it just one of those low points in the normal fluctuation in morale? The evidence not only helps me make my own judgment, but also helps define what you mean. Don't you think that defining what you mean is helpful with words like low morale?"

(Supervisor starts by understanding the subordinate's position. Then, after giving an example—always a helpful thing to do—the supervisor ends with a question to get a reaction.)

"Well, you might be right but I figured everybody knows what low morale is. And I figured that since I'm a section head you must have some confidence in my judgment. And I don't want to be spending all my time writing reports when I have plenty of other work to do. Besides, as I said, I didn't think you'd want to read all that stuff."

(Up to this point subordinate has not accepted supervisor's criticism.)

"Tom, I have plenty of confidence in your judgment or else you wouldn't be a section head. The point is, low morale can mean different things to different people. Let's reverse the situation for a moment. Suppose I told you that you're not supervising your men well enough. Now, everybody knows what supervising means. But wouldn't you want to know what I based this opinion on?"

(Supervisor reverses positions—a very helpful technique for enlarging the view—and again ends with a question to get a reaction.)

"Well, yes, I would. I'd want to know what you thought I was doing wrong."

"Of course, you would. And does your asking me this imply that you don't have confidence in my judgment?"

"No. It's just a question of getting a better understanding."

"Well then aren't I doing the very same thing you'd do if you were in my position?"

"I see what you mean and I'll try to be more specific from now on."

In the above conversation, the superior asked questions to make the subordinate think about the problem. As a result, the subordinate's misconceptions and basis for resistance were drawn out where they could be examined. Then, the superior reversed positions and again asked the subordinate to think about it. This takes a little more time initially but much less in the long run. And the resulting meeting of minds makes it well worth while.

To Change a Person's Mind, You Must Make Him Discard His Idea And Try Yours

As people move through life they build up a wardrobe of ideas and points of view. These ideas are comfortable. They fit well. They suit the taste of the individual and he feels at ease with them. Like an old shoe, they have become shaped to his contours.

He's reluctant to discard any of these ideas for something new. When he tries on new ideas they feel awkward. They're not cut quite right for him. He misses the security of the old ideas and sometimes scarcely recognizes himself when holding the new ones. So why should he give up the comfort and security of old ideas, particularly when they all fit together so well, for new ideas just because they seem to make a little more sense. After all, they just look better now but they may look worse tomorrow.

The truth is that he isn't likely to be swayed merely by logic to give up any of his ideas for new ones. As every good clothing salesman knows, a man doesn't begin to buy a suit until he tries it on. And a man doesn't begin to buy an idea until he sees how it mentally fits him.

So many people fail in their attempts to influence others simply because they do not get the other person to try on the ideas presented. All too often the person trying to influence focuses exclusively on the package he is presenting. He sets his ideas out neatly against a glistening background of irrefutable arguments. The whole pattern may seem irresistible to him largely because he is the one that's wearing it at the moment. The other person is viewing it at a distance and from that distance his own ideas seem preferable. Continuing the parallel with the clothing salesman, in order to sell your ideas you have to get the other person to take off his and try on yours so that he can see how he feels in them rather than merely how they look by themselves.

When you tell an idea to another person it is like holding up the suit for him to examine. He glances at it indifferently casually, but it doesn't have any personal meaning for him. As with the suit, you now have to get him to try the idea on, fit it to the contours of his mind. When he tries on the new idea and it feels comfortable to him, he will discard the old one. The question remains, How do you get the other person to try on your ideas?

Get the Other Person to Talk About Your Ideas

As you present your ideas in conversation, your listener sits in his own mental audience and observes your ideas as they flit by on the screen of his mind. He views passively whatever images your words suggest to him. But there is still distance between these ideas and himself. He may admire the ideas or be amused or repelled by them, but they are still something detached from him.

In order for them to become a part of his thinking he has to fit them into his conceptual framework. He has to decide where he stands with regard to them. He has to wonder how he would use them, how they would affect him, what he should do about them. And before he can do this he has to talk about them.

When he talks about your ideas he fits them into his own

familiar patterns of words. He sees how they go with his other ideas. In order to translate your ideas into his own words, rather than just repeating your words, he has to separate the ideas from the words themselves. He has to get the feel of them. He has to understand their implications.

When he talks about your ideas he makes them his own. This does not mean that he is disclaiming you as the source of the ideas, but merely that he is subscribing to their worthwhileness. He has made them his own in that he has experienced them as a part of his thinking and feeling rather than merely as a part of his hearing. And this means also that he has made over the ideas. They have become something just a little bit different in his mind from what they are in yours. For no idea is ever grasped exactly the same way by any two people, simply because people experience the whole of reality differently from each other, just by virtue of being different and of having had different experiences.

When your listener has experienced your ideas as a force to be adjusted to, reckoned with, used or rejected, you have gotten through to him. Anything short of this is merely a buzz of language, a passing in review of images, an alternating of talking—but not a mental interaction, not a meeting of minds. Think about this in the next conversation you participate in or observe. When one person presents an idea and the other person does not talk about it, there is no real penetration.

Your Questions Should Have A Purpose

Skillfully put questions can guide another person's thinking far more persuasively than the most logical argument. Moving another person's thinking by questioning is probably as old as human discourse. Socrates achieved fame by developing it to a fine art.

To bring the other person's thinking to the desired conclusion the line of questioning has to be oriented toward the goal in mind. Don't just question randomly when you are trying to convince. For each question you ought to have an idea in mind which you are trying to verify.

Let's take a closer look at the use of questioning to move another person's thinking. We can do this by observing for a moment an interview between a sales manager and one of his salesmen who doesn't seem to be producing as well as he should. After a little social interchange the sales manager comes to the point.

"Bob, I wanted to talk to you about your sales volume. It's fallen off in the last three months and I think we'd better find out why."

"I don't know why it is but the customers just seem to be buying less of our stuff. Maybe business in general has fallen off."

(The salesman, while admitting some uncertainty, tends to blame the fall-off on his customers.)

"I know for a fact that business in general hasn't fallen off. And while things may have changed in your territory, I think it would be worth while to explore the way you're handling your job, don't you?"

(The manager concedes the possibility of what the salesman is suggesting as a way of encouraging the salesman, in turn, to accept the manager's thinking.)

"It's all right with me. But I think I'm doing my job."

(The salesman is a little defensive.)

"Well, let's take a closer look. I've been looking at your reports for the last six months and I notice that you're giving very little time to going after new business. You seem to be spending almost all your time calling on our regular customers. Don't you think it would be worth while to go after new business?"

(Manager starts with the facts and ends with a question to get a reaction.)

"Yes, I do. But the trouble is that my territory is too large. I've got too many accounts to call on. I've got to service my regular customers or else my competition is going to come in. I've got to hold on to what I've got and I just don't seem to have any time left after I call on my regular accounts."

"Well, let's take a closer look at that. I noticed from your reports that you're calling on Acme twice a month."

(Manager stays with the facts. Implied question at end is, How come?)

"Acme is my best customer. It would be quite a blow if I lost them. And my competition is breathing down my neck."

"Of course, we certainly don't want to lose them. Are they pretty happy with us?"

(Manager acknowledges agreement on one point and continues questioning.)

"Sure they are. We're getting almost all their business and I'm on pretty good terms with their people."

"That's fine. Now, what do you think would happen if you cut down your visits to them to once a month instead of twice?"

"I don't know. They like to see me around there regularly."

"I appreciate that, but considering the way they feel about our products and your relationship with them do you think we'd actually lose any business?"

"No, I guess not."

"Then that would leave you one call a month you could use elsewhere, right?"

"Yes. I see what you're getting at."

"Now, I also see from your reports that you've been calling on National only once every two months."

"Well they only give me about a quarter of the business that Acme does."

"That's true, but isn't their potential even greater than Acme's, only they're giving most of it to our competition?"

"Yeah, that's right. I haven't been able to increase my share there."

"Well, wouldn't it make sense to increase your calls there, where the potential is, so that you could get some more business?"

"I see what you mean. Maybe I better look over my other accounts as well."

"That's an excellent idea. What plan will you follow in doing this?"

(Manager asks question to make salesman articulate the general procedure he will follow.)

"Well, I'll see if I can cut down the number of calls on those accounts where I'm getting all or most of the business, where I'm really in solid. And I'll use the extra calls for accounts where the potential is greater than what I'm now getting, and for getting new customers."

"That's really using your head. And I think it'll step up your sales a great deal."

(Manager praises salesman to encourage his active thinking.)

In the above discussion the manager moved the salesman's thinking by asking him a question at every step of the way. The manager did not try to pound arguments into the salesman. He didn't harangue the salesman with his own ideas. Instead, he presented some ideas and made the salesman think about them, by questioning him after each idea. The manager made the salesman's mind reach out and take each idea from his own mind and work on it. And the questions were oriented toward the manager's purpose. This is how minds are made to meet.

Asking Questions Is a Way Of Holding The Initiative

When you ask questions you are really leading the other person's thinking. You point his mind in a particular direction and prod him to move to find an answer. A question is, in effect, a request to think about a subject.

Many declarative statements are really questions in disguise. For example, "I expected to see you at the party last night," although not in question form, really means, Why weren't you at the party last night? And virtually any sentence that begins with something like, "Now, I don't know what you think about this, but I think—" also asks, "What do you think about this?"

A statement you make about which there could be some difference of opinion, contains within it an implicit question, a request for the other person's position. For example, you say "Underneath it all in spite of his seeming crudeness and selfishness, I still think Harry is a fundamentally decent and good hearted person." Your comment calls for an indication of agreement or disagreement from the other person. Your statement has hanging on the end of it the unspoken question, What do you think? And such unspoken questions, like their spoken counterparts, direct the other person's thinking.

The role of the questioner is at times deceptive. He seems to be the dependent one, appealing for information or advice, the one ready to listen to the voice of authority. But actually he is taking command of the other person's mind, driving it in his desired direction, making it think at his bidding in the direction that he chooses.

Questions are stimulating to the mind. Look at the radio and TV quiz craze. People love to be asked questions. One of the most famous lines in poetry is a question, "To be or not to be."

Perhaps questions are so stimulating to so many people because they give people something to think about. People would often like the pleasure of using their minds constructively, and the question organizes the problem for them, sets the task. The question says, Think of this.

Let's watch a salesman hold the initiative through questions. He is just getting down to business in the buyer's office.

"Tests have shown that our product outlasts our nearest competitor by 15 per cent, and other competitors by much more than that. Yet our price is the same. Therefore, our products will save you money in the long run. How do you feel about saving this money?"

"Well, naturally, I'd like to save money but we're all set up with the product we're using. Our men are used to it. In other words, we're generally satisfied with what we've got now."

"When you say you're satisfied does this mean that you don't have any trouble at all?"

"We have a little trouble occasionally, nothing to be really concerned about. But nothing is perfect, anyway."

"Sure, nothing is perfect. But we try to keep the trouble down to a minimum. What kind of trouble are you having?"

"Nothing serious, but I was looking at the records recently and we don't get as much life out of a product as I had expected."

"How much life are you getting?"

"About three months."

"Three months. That's a quarter less than the life you should be getting. Ours lasts four months. Wouldn't you like to extend the life of your product?"

"Oh, sure. But there's more to it than that. First of all, this is only a minor item in our production. And I don't like to upset the procedure. It would mean a new set of operating instructions. I don't want the fellows on the floor to get confused and start messing things up."

"I can understand your not wanting to get things messed up, but I wonder if this is likely to happen. How long have you been using your present product?"

"Oh, about three years."

"Then about three years ago you had a changeover from another brand you were using to the brand you're now using. Is that right?"

"Yes, that's right. But what are you getting at?"

"I'm just trying to look at the record. How much trouble was there in that change-over?"

"Well, let's see now. There wasn't really any trouble that I can remember. Once or twice when things went wrong somebody blamed it on the new product but it was quickly straightened out."

"Then aren't you paying twenty-five per cent more to prevent some trouble that isn't even likely to happen, from your own experience?"

"Well, maybe I am worrying a little too much about what the fellows will say. Frankly, I've been a little annoyed about the short life of the product but to avoid trouble I figured I'd just live with it. Suppose you send me a trial package of your stuff and we'll see how it works out."

This salesman held the initiative all the way, through pointed questioning. The initial questions stirred the buyer's mind to activity rather than leaving him in a state of inertia, with an unwillingness to consider anything different. Subsequent questions moved the buyer's thinking until he, himself, confronted with the illogic of his position, reached out for a trial order.

Make Questioning a Habit

Keep in mind that questions are used for much more than just getting information. Questions are also used to get another person to take a position, make a commitment. It is this use of questioning that arouses more active thinking and moves it along.

Asking questions of a person requests him to put his thinking into words. The very process of verbally articulating one's thoughts clarifies them. It holds them up to scrutiny to see if they're realistic. Flaws in thinking are exposed.

When you are trying to sell an idea, and somewhere along the way you say something that amounts to, If I can show you how this idea will benefit you, will you buy it? the other person will either say yes or reveal other reservations. He has to think his way through to a position of agreement, or crystallize his objections. This bringing of thinking into the open helps minds get closer together.

In your conversations get into the habit of questioning; not just to get facts but to activate the other person's thinking, particularly about your ideas. When you make a statement don't consider it complete unless you have also asked for a reaction to that statement. It isn't enough that what you say is information-bearing. It must be mind-stimulating as well. And the question part of your comment is the mind stimulator.

When you are trying to persuade another person to adopt your position, don't just ask questions at random. Ask yourself first, "What information do I need to build my case?" Then ask questions to elicit this information from the other person. When you have done so then ask questions to make him take a position.

As you get into the habit of asking questions you will find your conversations richer in information and more stimulating both to the other person and yourself, as your minds become more active.

9

Dealing with Resistance

Opposition is a Sign of Involvement

In order to persuade someone to your way of thinking it is necessary that he first pass through a stage of resistance. The resistance arises from his having to give up the position he already has. He may listen to you, comprehend what you say, even do what you say. But listening or even complying for the moment doesn't necessarily mean that he accepts what you say. After all, he can do what you ask simply because he wants to please you, without necessarily adopting your ideas.

But taking over your ideas requires a readjustment of a number of other associated ideas he has. Your thinking has to be made to fit into the whole train of his associated thinking. And pressure on him to change his thinking is going to arouse some resistance.

If his mind were empty to begin with, he might readily accept your ideas. They would rush in to fill the vacuum. But peo-

124

ple's minds are not empty. They have ideas and positions on just about everything. Even if many of these positions have never been put into words, they exist implicitly, following from other ideas or feelings.

For example, suppose you were trying to persuade someone to go for an annual medical check-up. He may nod, agree that it's a good idea, and then not move to do anything about it. Within him is an oppositional force to this idea. He may be afraid of the findings. He may feel that there can't be anything wrong with him since if there were he would feel pain or experience some other symptom. He may shy away from the discomfort he anticipates from a thorough medical examination. And he might not want to spend the money or give up the time.

When you present to him the idea of yearly medical examinations he doesn't argue. He doesn't want to engage you in argument because he knows that on the basic of logic he would lose; and if logic were the basis of his action he would have to go. Therefore, he avoids engagement. He agrees. He gives lip service. He terminates discussion of the subject by giving outward indications of acceptance. In effect, he has cut off your channel of persuasion.

On the other hand, when he opposes you, marshals arguments contrary to yours, he leaves himself open to convincing. Now something within him is responding to your ideas. Some part of him feels that what you are saying makes sense and another part of him—the part that doesn't want to go—is fighting against your arguments. His resistance, his struggle to convince you of the opposite, is a sign that he is fully involved in considering your position. He isn't comfortable with his own. He knows deep down that it doesn't make sense but fights to hold it anyway by trying to convince you as a way of convincing himself. In any case the channel of persuasion is open. He is responsive to your arguments even though the response at the moment is oppositional. One part of him is in conflict with another.

When Agreement Is Given Without Thought Press For A Commitment To Action

When you are trying to convince someone, and your arguments are so readily accepted as to make you suspect that he is agreeing only to put you off, greater pressure is needed. While it might seem that pressure is needed only when opposition is vehement, and is out of place when compliance is expressed, just the opposite is true.

Vehement opposition should be drawn out until its force is spent. But ready assent needs to be tested, and if necessary the other person must be provoked into revealing the opposition concealed by his assent.

This testing can be done by asking for a commitment to action. For example, in the case of the suggested medical examination discussed above, after obtaining agreement the other person might be asked when and where he intends to take the exam. If he commits himself to time and place, he has probably been won over. But if he becomes irritated and wants to leave the subject, focus on his reaction, as a way of bringing out his reservation. Suggest to him that his annoyance may indicate some reluctance he still has and that you feel it would be helpful if he would tell you his reasons for avoiding going.

It should be kept in mind that when you apply this kind of pressure you run the risk of alienating the other person and not succeeding anyway. Before using this method you ought to ask yourself whether it really is your business to push the other person into doing what you want. Is it realistically necessary or are you just trying to have your way? Perhaps his way is after all the better way, at least for him. In the case of the medical exam it might be more proper for you to merely suggest, perhaps even to urge a bit, but not to press hard. This depends of course on the circumstances.

In the case of a manager instructing a subordinate it is the manager's responsibility to see that the subordinate complies.

And where there is resistance it has to be overcome with whatever method is called for by the form of the resistance.

The manager when getting too casual an agreement might ask for a further commitment by requesting the subordinate to tell specifically when or how he intends to do it. Similarly, a salesman has to try to overcome objections however he best can, because selling is his job. When the prospect nods without caring, the salesman should ask for an order; and when this is put off the salesman should explore further. Why isn't the prospect ready? The prospect replies that he has to think about it some more. When should the salesman call for an answer? The prospect answers that he isn't sure this is right for him. What are his reservations? This pressing for specifics is a way of engaging the prospect so that the channels of persuasion are opened.

Inner Conflict Can Intensify Opposition

People are frequently in conflict with themselves, desiring mutually exclusive things. And wanting to move in two different directions at the same time is accompanied by a feeling of anxiety, the anxiety that one will miss something. Moving toward either goal means giving up the other.

At the same time one can't remain immobile, for that means giving up both goals. So a start is made in one direction, and as movement in this direction continues the opposite goal becomes more distant and anxiety rises over giving it up. The individual then back-tracks and starts toward the first goal only to encounter again a rise in anxiety as the first goal recedes. The result is indecision and vacillation between goals. Nothing is accomplished and the individual remains in a state of discomfort arising from the conflict, until he makes up his mind.

Now suppose you are trying to persuade someone to adopt a course of action and your suggestion appeals to him. Suppose also that he had been headed in an opposite direction and still somewhat desires this. Your suggestion arouses a conflict within him between moving in your direction and moving in his original one. He wants to do both of these at the same time.

If he were left to his own devices at this point he might vacillate between the two courses of action. You are applying pressure in one direction and his anxiety mounts as he feels himself being pulled from the opposite goal that he also wants. So he mentally digs his heels in and pulls back against you.

He becomes more vehement. He is now fighting not only his own partial tendency to move in your direction but your urging as well. His voice may become louder, his speech quicker. He may jump from one argument to another trying to pile them up as quickly as possible. He may even cut off the discussion abruptly.

Such intense opposition may very well indicate a wish to adopt the very course of action that is being opposed. Shakespeare's line, "Methinks the lady doth protest too much," illustrates this. Opposition is often a sign of interest in doing what the other person wants.

When Opposition Is Vehement, Become Neutral

When opposition is intense, indicating a conflict within the other person, it is pointless for you to apply your counter arguments with equal or greater vehemence since this only forces the other person to maintain a strong stand so as to keep the conflict unresolved, since moving either way is too threatening to him.

At this point you should abandon your pressure. This will cause the other person to abandon his counter pressure, and will place him in an anxious state again. Actually, your pressure temporarily relieved his anxiety since it removed his conflict for the moment. Instead of arguing with himself, which is anxiety-provoking, he now could argue with you.

Once you take off the pressure and retreat to a neutral position he has to take over both positions again, for and against, and is back arguing with himself. And this also means that the force within him that's on your side, and that you had previously taken over and now abandoned, is back in strength again.

For the moment you want to keep it this way. And then you gradually want to strengthen the force favoring you, and weaken the other. Remain neutral. Be objective. You might recapitulate the arguments against your own position and ask him to sum up the factors favoring your stand. In effect you're reversing positions for the moment. Then ask him to evaluate each point, pro and con. Be sure to be generous in conceding strength to the other side. This will encourage him to do the same.

Gradually, as you explore in this manner, the irrational or emotional factors will evaporate and opposition based on unreasonable fears will diminish. At the same time he will become more comfortable in your position as he talks about its strong points. If your position is realistically better than his for him, he is now likely to adopt it. In any case he is now more likely to be evaluating the situation on its real merits and less likely to be guided by anxiety or irritation or any other emotion in making his decision.

Rational And Irrational Opposition

When two people in a discussion are in opposition to each other, more is happening than just two different viewpoints being explained. Each is also resisting the other.

The process of resisting is common to many events in an individual's life going back to infancy. The child may resist the discipline of his parents, the rules of his teacher, the requests of his friends; and, as he grows up, the demands of his job, the wishes of his mate, and the customs of society.

Resistance can become a habit, a way of responding, completely apart from the facts of a given situation. And like all habits, the strength of the resisting habit may range from zero all the way up to intense opposition to just about everything, where one resists for the sake of resisting.

In discussions in which two people oppose each other there are often both rational and irrational elements. The rational basis for difference in viewpoints lies in the different facts each has and in different tastes and values. The irrational basis for conflict lies outside the facts of the case, and is untouched by the immediate topic. It may lie in the wish to oppose or in some counter-wish or fear that exists within the individual, moving him in the opposite direction. For example, a buyer may resist a salesman's presentation not on the basis of what's offered but simply because the salesman represents a big company while the buyer favors the underdog, the small company.

The wish to oppose operates in a variety of ways. For example, when given instructions or when restricted in some manner an individual may become oppositional because of a need to assert independence, or a resentment of all discipline. Similarly, one may want to resist certain individuals while desiring to please others, completely apart from the facts. Also, irritability increases the wish to resist, while pleasurable feelings diminish it. This is why the smart wife saves her demands till after her husband has enjoyed a good dinner. At the very moment when your own wish to oppose is operating you may ascribe such irrational resistance to the other person for opposing your arguments.

Signs Of Irrational Opposition

When you encounter opposition you have to evaluate this opposition for its rational and irrational elements in order to know how to deal with it. If it's largely rational then it becomes strictly a matter of weighing the facts on both sides and of determining also whether the other person's different viewpoint stems from different values. If his position is as soundly based as yours it is pointless to try to convert him; and if his case is still sounder than yours, your persistence may represent your own irrationality.

On the other hand if his opposition is largely irrational,

weighing the facts won't work since he's not being guided by the facts. He simply wants to oppose for reasons he wishes to conceal from you or even from himself. He may oppose simply because he's afraid to change from any present position. Or he may be in conflict, wanting what you suggest without being willing to give up what he has now, even though they are mutually exclusive. Or he may resent others trying to influence him. Or he may dislike you personally.

But whatever his reasons are, his resistance remains irrational as long as it is not based on the facts in the case. It is therefore pointless to argue the facts in the face of irrational opposition.

In order to deal with irrational opposition one has to first recognize its presence.

Five Signs Of Irrational Opposition

1. VEHEMENCE. When an individual opposes an idea with more intensity than the situation warrants it means that he isn't quite comfortable in the position he holds. This intensity is really an attempt to discharge some strong feelings he has.

As described earlier, he might be in conflict, wanting to move in both directions at once. Part of him may want to adopt the very idea he is opposing. In order to resist his own inclinations he exerts greater oppositional force to convince both his opponent and himself.

The vehemence may also be a discharge of anger from another source, or an expression of animosity towards the opponent in the discussion. In any case, the vehemence likely represents irrational opposition, resistance unrelated to the facts of the discussion.

2. UNRESPONSIVENESS. When an individual clings to his fixed position of resistance without considering the counter arguments offered him he must have a wish to hold this position for reasons not revealed in the discussion. He isn't open to new information to help him find the best conclusion. He simply wants to keep what he has because it serves some private need

of his. This is irrational opposition in the sense that he is not responsive to the rationality introduced by the other person.

3. IRRELEVANCE. The introduction of irrelevant arguments to buttress an oppositional stand implies a lack of relevant ones. For if relevant arguments were available, they would be used. The resisting individual, in offering unrelated or picayune reasons for holding to his position, is trying to conceal the real ones.

People's behavior will make much more sense to you if you keep in mind that they act in the direction of the stronger reason. When they give weak ones it's only because they don't want to reveal the true reasons. Irrelevance then indicates the presence of some hidden, irrational basis for opposition.

4. RATIONALIZING. Trying to make it seem logical to hold the contrary position when it isn't logical is again an attempt at concealment. One may exaggerate the importance of his arguments, or minimize the importance of the other person's, or use guesses or wishes as though they were facts, in order to give a rational facade to one's position. Again this is irrational in that one is acting on motives not introduced into the discussion. And the chances are that when motives are concealed there is an irrational element. For if the person were being secretive for logical reasons he would generally indicate explicitly that he doesn't want to reveal his reasons.

5. OBJECTION-HOPPING. When an idea is proposed and the person opposing the idea jumps from one objection to another, not absorbing the answers to his objections, these objections have very little to do with the real reason for his opposition.

If an objection were really important to him he would listen carefully to the counter argument. And it is very likely that he would re-phrase the counter argument in his own words in his attempt to make it part of his thinking. In other words, he would dwell on it, try to grasp it firmly.

People do not change positions immediately upon hearing a logical reason for doing so, no matter how good the case for changing is. Even though the evidence clearly favors changing positions, people are hesitant to do it in a single jump. They want to work it over in their minds, make sure they understand it and are doing the right thing. They want to thread their way cautiously to the new position, surveying the ground around them to make sure it's firm.

This means that when an individual quickly leaves an objection after you have offered a convincing counter argument, and jumps to another objection, the first one really didn't mean much to him. He didn't leave the first objection because your counter argument convinced him. He simply didn't care about it. If he had cared he would have stayed with his objection and your counter-argument for a while. He would have thought it through, re-phrasing it, commenting on it, relinquishing his objection slowly, by degrees, as though it took some struggle within him to let go of it. This struggle is your sign that he has really changed from one position to another.

In general then when you are trying to influence thinking and are faced with opposition, watch for the following: an overly intense emotional reaction; departure from the straight line of reasoning; and a lack of absorbing of your ideas. When you encounter any of these you might as well abandon your current line of argument since it will not be bearing upon the other person's real basis of resistance.

Handling Irrational Opposition

Overcoming rational opposition is a matter of logical argument. Two people in opposition look at the arguments on both sides and decide which side has greater merit. When you encounter rational opposition you simply have to have a superior case for your side if you want to influence the thinking of the other person. You can't expect to sell your ideas when not buying them makes more sense. You have to either get more ammunition or give up.

Of course, you may reach an impasse with the other person not because the facts are on his side or because your arguments are weak, but simply because his tastes and values are different from yours. You and he do not attach the same importance to the same things. His not buying your ideas doesn't necessarily mean that his case is stronger nor that his opposition is irrational, but merely that he feels differently than you about the same things.

For example, you can't convince a man to put his money into a high income—high risk venture by painting a glowing picture of the profit he could make, when security is more important to him. You may prefer to take the risk for the potentially handsome reward, while he simply is content with a low but safe yield on his investment. Neither one makes more sense than the other. It's a question of personal value, whether the individual considers potential gain or security more important.

Irrational opposition is a very different matter. Here the cards are not on the table. The real reasons are hidden. There is an imperviousness to logical argument. No matter how brilliant the reasoning, it simply doesn't get through. Special steps have to be taken to deal with this irrational opposition before logic can be brought into play.

Three Ways Of Dealing With Irrational Opposition

1. EXPRESS UNDERSTANDING. Although everyone acts irrationally now and then, and some more than others, one's own irrationality is difficult to face. It's frightening. It touches off anxiety and guilt. Substantial citizens who would not cheat at cards or steal your wallet or even stick you with a dinner check will resort to all kinds of deception to deny their own irrationality. Let's take a closer look at irrationality to see why it's so self-intimidating.

Irrationality is the acting on inner impulses without regard for outer circumstances. One does what one wants at the moment in disregard of the consequences. Instead of responding to the total reality, both within oneself and in the world around one, only the inner world guides action for the irrational moments.

Impulses may be kind and generous, a desire to give and to help. They may be harmless pleasure-seeking ones—to eat a fattening desert, whistle at a pretty girl, or buy a new hat or fishing rod. They may be larger in scope—to climb a mountain, go on a trip, find sex or indulge in any other pleasure-seeking activity. And they may range from cheating and stealing through assault and sexual perversion to murder. The inner world is a most active one, but man has controls to suppress impulses and to help him express them in socially acceptable ways. Man's reason tells him what he can do, what he should do, and what will hurt him.

Man's self-control is the only thing that prevents his venting of impulses that might get him into trouble. People who are confident that their self-control is stronger than their impulses are not afraid of getting into trouble. However, when the impulse threatens to overwhelm the control, anxiety sets in as a warning signal.

Now when people chronically worry about their impulses getting out of control, whether consciously or unconsciously, any slight irrationality raises for them the frightening question, Is the wall of control beginning to crack? If a small, harmless impulse gets away from them, might not a larger, dangerous one do the same?

When a little impulse gets out of hand, rather than accepting it as a harmless self-indulgence, they become afraid that they might be heading toward a release of some dangerous impulse. As a result they deny that they merely catered to a whim and instead develop some logical justification for gratifying the small, harmless impulse.

One may deny irrationality either by developing a logical justification for doing what one is really doing on impulse, or by suppressing the impulse even to the extent of moving to the opposite behavior. For example, suppose a person has an abiding impulse to control others, to dominate. He may express this directly and justify it by advancing the thesis that people are not dependable. They have to be told just what to do and be supervised closely. Or he may deny the impulse possibly by moving to the opposite extreme. He may become submissive, unable to say no to anyone.

The practical question now is, When someone employs defenses—vehemence, unresponsiveness, irrelevance, rationalizing, objection-hopping—to obscure his real motivation, how can one reach him? The answer lies in gradual, easy, comfortable uncovering of the real motivation.

The layer of rationality can't suddenly be stripped away and impulses exposed or else the individual will become anxious or angry. The whole purpose of the conversation—and possibly the relationship itself—will be lost in the resulting emotional repercussions. He must be brought gradually to face the truth, moved along a little at a time. He must adjust by degrees to the uncovering of his feelings as one adjusts to sudden darkness or brightness, to noxious odors which seem to disappear merely because one has gotten used to them, and to new surroundings whose inconveniences seem much greater at first than they later turn out to be.

And the way can be made much easier for him by your accepting sympathetically the very irrationality that he is trying to hide. When you show a willingness to face it with equanimity and understanding he will be encouraged to reveal it, to make it an open part of the conversation. But if you indicate to him that everything he says will be subjected to the cold glare of logic and that he will be judged accordingly, the barricade will be thrown up.

When encountering opposition, the first thing to do is to express acceptance of the other person's viewpoint. Now, acceptance does not mean merely comprehension, that you heard what he said. Nor does it mean agreement with his position.

Your acceptance of another person's position means that you understand the way he feels and that you are not expecting him to necessarily conform to your way of reacting. You are not trying to prove that yours must be the better way for him. It is merely what *you* would do; but he might choose something quite different for personal reasons that make sense to him, and that his way might be as good for him as yours is for you.

You are merely offering your thinking to him so that he might have an opportunity to choose it if he wishes. He can then decide for himself which would be better for him.

Even though an individual envelopes his impulses in a cloak of rationality to conceal them from others, and to make it appear as though he is acting with sensible concern for his environment, he may still be troubled by his inner motivations. He may be consciously unaware of these impulses and yet somewhere within him they are active and give rise to disturbing feelings.

When you express acceptance of his viewpoint, your acceptance spreads from the logical position he expounds to the troubling impulses within. He feels freer in revealing himself since you seem to understand that a certain amount of irrationality is a normal part of everyone's behavior. Your willingness to consider sympathetically the way he feels encourages him to reciprocate, to cooperate by looking at your position.

Let's take some examples. Suppose a friend who is facing an imminent surgical operation remarks to you that he is worried about it. It would be unkind to tell him that there is nothing to worry about, since in doing so you are implying that he is irrational for worrying. It would be more reassuring to begin with something like:

"I can appreciate your being anxious about the operation. Facing any operation is unpleasant. I'd probably feel the same way you do."

Then you might get him to talk a little more about it. Talk helps to release the uncomfortable pressure of anxiety or any other emotion. For example, ask him about the reason for the operation or what his doctor said. After he has done some talking you can then reassure him. For example you might say:

"You know, I've heard that modern procedures make this operation a pretty safe one and not as uncomfortable as you think. On a lot of these things the anticipation is worse than the actual experience."

Here we have the acceptance of anxiety, and its talking-out, rather than the dismissing of it as uncalled for.

Similarly, suppose an employee stalks angrily into his supervisor's office and says something like this:

"I'm fed up. I just found out that Joe Walters, who's doing the same job I am, is making a thousand a year more. I'm sick and tired of being pushed around. I've had it."

There is an irrational element in the employee's reaction, since he didn't stop to inquire of the supervisor why Joe Walters is making more money. There may be a good explanation, but he doesn't want to consider it.

Rather than immediately launching into an explanation for the salary difference it would be better for the supervisor to accept the subordinate's anger by saying something like:

"I can appreciate your being angry at this salary difference. You feel that we're taking advantage of you because we're paying you less than Walters."

This response by the supervisor is likely to disarm the subordinate. It makes the subordinate feel that the supervisor understands him, accepts his angry reaction as being natural, and suggests to him that perhaps the supervisor was not trying to hurt him in any way. He is likely to reply as follows:

"Yes, that's it. Why shouldn't I get paid the same as Walters if I'm doing the same thing?"

His taking a questioning position indicates that the subordinate is at least a little more receptive now to the supervisor's explanation, and the supervisor can give a reason at this point, or promise to explore the matter.

In general, when encountering opposition, begin by expressing your appreciation of the other person's feeling on the subject. And in expressing this appreciation, feed back to him your interpretation of his position. Keep in mind that feelings have to be accepted and understood. They are non-rational. They are not subject to logical scrutiny. It is pointless to try to decide whether a person should or should not be angry or anxious or happy. The feeling is there and it has to be dealt with separately from the ideas expressed. Only the ideas can be logically examined.

2. MAKE THE OTHER PERSON AWARE THAT HE IS RESISTING. Often someone may resist without being aware that he is resisting. He closes himself off. He doesn't respond to what's being said.

For example, in a sales interview the buyer may be non-committal, very reluctant about offering any kind of information, and remain silent, not indicating any reaction to the salesman's presentation. He neither agrees nor objects.

Although the buyer does not explicitly indicate opposition his non-participation is a form of resistance. Salesmen encountering this kind of situation are likely to feel frustrated, knowing they are not reaching the buyer.

This silent form of opposition is difficult to deal with because the resistance isn't verbalized, there isn't anything tangible to work on. Yet it is resistance all the same; for when someone is receptive, he reacts to the arguments presented, gives information freely, and asks questions.

In this case, the buyer may be unaware that he is resisting. After all he isn't opposing anything. He may think of opposition as an act against something and he isn't acting one way or the other. Actually, uncooperativeness is in itself a form of resistance.

It would be pointless for the salesman to pursue his line of argument since it is falling on a closed mind if not deaf ears. He needs to make the buyer aware that he is resisting, that there are perhaps elements of irrationality behind the opposition. At the same time, the salesman can't directly tell this to the buyer, since suddenly confronting the buyer with his own irrational behavior is likely to anger him. He'll protest that he hasn't said anything to indicate opposition on his part. This, of course, is true but the opposition is indicated by what he didn't say, rather than what he said.

In order to focus the buyer's attention on his own resistance and do so gently, the salesman might say something like:

"You don't seem very willing to discuss my product with me and I'm wondering if there is something my company or I have done that annoyed you."

It's hard for the buyer to take offense at a statement that shows concern for his feelings. At the same time, the salesman's statement draws the buyer's attention to his own uncooperative behavior. The statement also calls for an explanation from the buyer regarding his uncooperativeness.

He may deny that he bears any resentment and continue to resist. But in a large proportion of cases the buyer, now that his attention has been drawn to his feelings, will recognize that he is bringing into the situation resentment from other sources. As a result, he is likely to thaw out and enter into the sales interview. This increased participation may then lead to his bringing out his real objections and to his actively considering the salesman's arguments.

3. EVALUATE THE OTHER PERSON'S OBJECTIONS WITH HIM. Going one step further, when the person resisting does so openly but does not give reasons, merely saying that he disagrees, ask him what his reservations are. After he faces the fact that he is opposing you, you have to bring out the reason for it. You might ask: "What are your reservations?" or, "Could you tell me something more about why you disagree?" or, "What are your objections?"

Once an objection has been brought out it has to be examined carefully. It has to be analyzed for the sense it makes. It may not be as important as it first seems, or it may not even apply at all. And it has to be compared with the arguments on the other side to see which is stronger. You have to determine if an objection can really stand up under close scrutiny.

The trouble is that too many people are afraid to pursue a close examination of an objection; and here is where their dealing with opposition falls apart. Rather than coming to grips with an objection they retreat to repeating their arguments. They're afraid to dwell on the other person's objection for fear that talking about it will make it grow larger. Actually, the opposite usually results. With discussion, the emotional elements are discharged and the objection diminishes to its logical value.

No matter how sound your arguments are they can't have a decisive effect until they are placed side by side with the other person's objections so that he can see which has the greater weight. And you can't place them beside each other until you clearly define the basis of his resistance.

If he doesn't make his objection explicit, you must guide him toward this before you can ask for a conclusion based on your argument. Yet so many people fail to influence others simply because instead of exploring objections, they keep repeating their own ideas. Your argument alone will not persuade. You must first unearth his objections, demolish them, and replace them with your point of view.

For example, suppose you had presented the benefits of a particular course of action to someone and he demurred on the ground that it was too much trouble. Rather than emphasizing again all that will be gained it would be much better at this point to explore just what trouble is really involved.

As the discussion about the trouble is pursued, what he considered trouble might boil down to something much less difficult than he thought it would be. This might then diminish the objection to the point where it isn't strong enough to stop him from doing as you suggest.

Similarly, if a salesman is presenting a particular line of merchandise to the buyer of a retail store, and the buyer objects that he has too much inventory, presenting him with the benefits of the new line isn't likely to be very effective at this point. His mind is blocked from absorbing your benefits. Until the block is disposed of he doesn't want to listen.

It would be much better now to explore what he means by too much inventory. Does he really mean that he doesn't want to increase his inventory under any circumstances or is it that he is afraid of buying more merchandise that won't move. If he were assured of getting quick turnover on some new merchandise, would he put some money into it or would he be content to remain with a small volume of sales from slow-moving merchandise?

His opposition may be partly based on a sensible estimate that he is overloaded. However, his resistance may have acquired additional force from anger at finding himself in an overloaded position, and a tendency to focus this anger on the salesman as though he were responsible for it. Actually, this salesman may have had nothing to do with the buyer's overloaded situation; and even if he had sold some or all of the merchandise to the buyer, from a rational point of view the buyer should judge the salesman's new idea on its own merits.

If the buyer should let out some of his anger by saying something like: "That's the trouble with you fellows. You're always loading me up with more stuff than I can move," so much the better. In this case, the salesman should continue to draw out the feeling by getting the buyer to talk some more about it, rather than refuting it. As the buyer talks, he is actually discharging some of the force behind his own opposition.

It's important to keep in mind that resistance is often based on a combination of rational and irrational elements. Brought into the light of discussion the rational element will maintain its dimensions. It will remain as important as it ever was. But the irrational element, similarly exposed, will tend to evaporate. The force it had in the dark of the individual's interior dies out when brought to light. As a result of discussing the resistance its force becomes reduced to the strength of the rational element.

Of course, if the rational element alone is enough to sustain the other person's position, he won't be influenced by your argument. But often it's the irrational addition that makes the difference, maintaining the opposition in the face of your arguments; and once the irrational portion is removed your arguments may prevail.

The Key Points In Dealing With Opposition

To sum up, your dealing with the other person's opposition should start with your expression of sympathetic understanding of the way he feels. This may include your feeding back to him your interpretation of his viewpoint as a way of demonstrating your understanding. This should be followed by a progressive drawing out and clarifying of his resistance.

When his resistance takes the form of abandoning the discussion by agreeing in an uncaring manner, press for a commitment to test his agreement. And if he puts you off or evades, continue to ask for specifics about his intentions as a way of drawing out his reservations.

On the other hand, when opposition is overly intense abandon pressure and become neutral. Be objective. Concede the merits of the opposing arguments as a way of encouraging him to acknowledge the strong points of your position. If possible, get him to try your position by asking him to recapitulate your arguments.

You may first have to make him aware that he is resisting, as in the case of the other person's minimal participation in the conversation. Or you may start further along, where the other person has brought out his objections but they need further delineating. Whatever portion is still in the dark has to be brought to light before you can expect your arguments to have effect.

In the case of objection-hopping, where the other person jumps to another objection as soon as you have answered the preceding one, it means that he hasn't brought out the really significant one. After answering a few of his front objections, rather than continuing to chase him around, it would be better to focus his attention on the fact that he is evading facing his real objection. You might do this by saying something like:

"While I realize that these objections you brought up are important and need to be answered, I have a feeling that there is something still more important bothering you."

In a number of cases, the other person might want to conceal his real objection and would deny your suggestion. But often he will suddenly realize that he isn't bringing out the main problem and that he might just as well do this so that you and he can come to grips with it.

In general, when you encounter opposition you have to examine for the presence of any irrational element. If this is present the other person has to be made aware of it so that he can exclude it, and weigh only his rational opposition against your arguments.

10

Measuring the Value of An Idea

Our Words Describe Our Reactions Rather Than The Objective Reality

As Joe Jones strolls down the street, a pretty-faced, curvy, blonde girl crosses his path. He turns to watch her body gracefully move away from him, and whistles. He nudges his companion and says, "Boy, is she sexy!"

The language Joe uses implies that the sexiness is in the girl. Actually, he is describing his own sexual excitement. He can't experience the girl directly. He can only experience his reaction to the girl; and this is all he can describe. Yet Joe maintains the illusion that the sexual excitement resides in the girl, is a part of her, rather than starting in him as a result of his experiencing of her. The very words he uses suggests this to him; and in passing along to others his impression of the girl he is likely to stimulate this same illusion in them.

Like Joe, we all tend to use language as though we were describing reality rather than our experiencing of it. This misconception leads to a great deal of distortion in thinking and communicating. For when we talk or hear someone talk we deal with the words as representations of reality. It's as though the words correspond with what actually happens rather than merely representing one's experiencing of it. And when words are taken as representing the reality encountered we are likely to make errors corresponding to the difference between what really happened and what was experienced.

Language lends itself more to describing reactions than to describing what is observed, while mathematics more nearly reflects the objective reality. Since in describing our reaction we are really including a part of ourselves, the description isn't an accurate representation but rather a mixture of self and observed event. Conversation is full of these intrusions of self resulting in distortions of what was observed.

To keep our thinking straight we have to separate what we actually see and hear, from the way we experience it. And to properly evaluate information we receive from others, we have to discriminate between their personal impressions and what really happened. In Chapter 6 one of the uses described for feeding back is to separate the other person's observations from his interpretations. Discussed here are further methods for evaluating information from others, as well as techniques for dealing with our own tendency to fuse actions we observe with our wishes, expectations, and emotions.

Five Ways Of Keeping Your Thinking Straight

1 EXAMINE YOUR EXPECTATIONS BEFORE JUDGING. Man adapts to sustained stimulation. The city-dweller no longer hears the constant din that makes the rural visitor wonder how he could ever possibly live there. At the same time, people living in the countryside do not hear the cacophony of sound emanating from beetles, birds, frogs and other creatures. Whatever it may be, *what one is used to or expects becomes the norm and only the departures from the norm are noted.*

Sixty degrees temperature is considered warm in December and cold in August. The word, *expensive,* is used very differently by poor man and rich. And a strong man would call a task easy that would be considered very difficult by a weak man.

Similarly, a timid salesman might consider the same prospect tough that an aggressive salesman considers easy. In talking about the prospect the timid salesman is really describing his fear, while the aggressive salesman is expressing his confidence. An autocratic supervisor, expecting unquestioning obedience, might call the same subordinate a trouble-maker that another supervisor, more democratic in viewpoint, considers easy to get along with. Again these two supervisors are describing their individual reactions, rather than talking objectively about the subordinate.

A teacher who has a very bright class of pupils comes to expect more and might consider the above-average student at the bottom of his class as rather dull, while this same student might shine in the eyes of a teacher of a slow class. And an executive, in the midst of an austerity program, when budgets are being squeezed, might consider a particular expenditure extravagant and frivolous that he would, in a period of easy money, consider reasonable in cost and worthwhile.

A tense, nervous person seeking excitement might label a situation as boring and dull, while the same situation is considered interesting and stimulating by a calmer, more serene individual. Similarly, taste and smell are affected by the immediately preceding taste and smell. After continued exposure, one gets so used to a noxious or fragrant odor, that one no longer smells it. And a moderately sweet food tastes much less sweet if it follows a highly sweet one. Sometimes, when we look backward we seem to be making progress. But when we look ahead we seem to be standing still.

If a salesman complains to a manager that a particular prospect gave him a hard time, the manager ought to find out what happened specifically. Perhaps the salesman expected more encouragement and considered it a hard time merely because the prospect was not warm and friendly and encouraging. A salesman might talk about being on the verge of getting the order when he's nowhere near it. In his over-optimism the salesman may feel that because the prospect did not terminate the relationship he is about to buy.

How we view the world depends on our present set of expectations and wants, and on our emotional state. In observing an event we have to screen out these distorting influences in order to accurately see what's really happening.

An individual may unconsciously harbor a childish expectation that everything should go his way and that nothing should ever happen that is inconvenient for him. When something goes against him he mistakenly feels that someone has deliberately harmed him. It seems to nim that there has been a violation of the rules, of the way things should be. He can't accept the fact that inconveniences and setbacks are bound to arise without their being intended by anyone, and that the world isn't planneu to suit hiᵥ purposes.

For example, the individual may become enrageᴅ at having been given a dirty spoon in a restaurant. Because of his underlying expectation that others should be concerned only with him he feels that the waitress or management has deliberately done something bad to him. He bawls out the waitress for being so careless or inconsiderate. He forgets that, statistically, so many spoons per thousand are bound to be dirty because an eᴇror factor creeps into every large-scale operation. And since many of these spoons slip by accidentally and are distributed to patrons, sooner or later he is bound to get one.

Instead he attributes his dirty spoon to some malevolence on the part of the waitress or others involved, forgetting about the many times he accidentally inconvenienced others.

Here, the anger is not really at the dirty spoon but at the idea that something is not going the way he wants it to. His resentment at this violation of his world view that nothing untoward should ever happen to him, that everything should center around him, pours out on his dirty-spoon situation. And this anger is likely an accumulation of resentments that pile up continually because things keep happening in the world without regard for whether they're good or bad for him.

A good way to screen out distortions resulting from unrealistic expectations is to focus directly on them. When you are about to judge or criticize someone, first ask yourself what you expect of him. Putting into words your expectations will help you take a realistic view. You may be expecting too much or too little, and without first evaluating your expectations you may criticize too harshly or, on the other hand, make too many allowances.

Your expecting too much may stem from wishful thinking. Or you may be making too many allowances to avoid the unpleasantness of having to confront someone with his deficiencies, or to deny to yourself that your initial confidence in him was misplaced.

Similarly, when you're trying to sell an idea to someone, first ask yourself how you expect him to react, and why you expect this. Answering these questions will give you a better grasp of whether your idea is saleable, and of how best to present it.

Another way of focusing on your expectations is to ask yourself if others would neccessarily view the particular situation in the way that you do. You might search in your mind for other ways of viewing it. This will make your expectations stand out apart from the objective reality.

For example, if you see two children running in the same direction, one ten feet directly behind the other, and describe this as one child chasing the other, you have superimposed your personal reaction. Another person might describe the same scene as two children running to get somewhere, with one merely behind the other rather than pursuing him.

Check your observations to see if you can interpret the same situation in another way. If another interpretation is possible revise your description so that it corresponds to what you directly observe. After awhile objective observation will become a habit.

There is no harm in adding your personal reactions but you should at least know where observation ends and interpretation begins.

2. QUANTIFY DESCRIPTIONS. When someone describes a situation to us we have to get beyond the adjective to find out how much of that characteristic is present. It's not enough to know that something is strong or durable or economical or tasty or desirable. We want to know how strong, how durable, how economical, how tasty or how desirable something is. We need to *quantify*, find its value.

Someone may say about another person, he's always complaining. If the listener does not question this, attempt to quantify it; he gets an impression of the second person as being a chronic complainer when this may be wholly inaccurate. The first person may just become angry at any complaint and exaggerate his experience with it, magnifying the complaining. The question, How often has he complained in the past three months and what did he complain about each time? might reveal that the complainer brought some unpleasant matter to the attention of the first person just three times in those three months and each time with justification.

A customer may complain to a salesman, "You're always late with your deliveries. How can we carry on a business when we don't know when we're getting merchandise from you?" The salesman might get a little frightened if he accepts this at face value, and disagree in general terms that his company is late all the time. It would be much wiser, particularly if he knows otherwise, to first express understanding of the other person's feeling and then to *quantify*. The salesman might do this by replying with something like, "I can appreciate your getting annoyed at that last late shipment but, honestly, how often have our shipments been late during the past year?" Exploration might reveal four late shipments during the entire year, two of which were late only one day on a thirty-day order; and the one day latenesses to be of no consequence anyway.

A student may complain to his teacher that the homework assignments are excessive, that he doesn't have time to complete them. Again, the feelings of the student may be affecting his appraisal in that he may not want to study and as a result, any amount of homework beyond the very limited amount that the student is willing to accept becomes excessive. Here, the teacher needs to *quantify* the situation by exploring with the student how much time he has been spending on the assignments and how much time he considers appropriate for homework.

Get into the habit of quantifying any descriptive information you receive. Is this information dependent on the subjective experiencing of the person giving it? Or is it completely unaffected by his reactions so that it stands alone as factual?

When someone tells you that a prospective employee changed jobs often, you really only know that the communicator of this information considers it often. His standards may be much different from yours. But it is easy for you to fall into the trap of taking these same words, applying your standard, and then forming an erroneous conclusion, since you will be measuring from your personal standard rather than from his. The important question here is, How often? The fact of holding four jobs in six years stands apart from any personal standards.

Similarly, how sick is sick? How late is late? How fast is fast? And when money is to be saved in the long run, how long is the run and how much money is involved.

A good rule of thumb in trying to quantify is to get a number or quantity designation in place of an adjective or adverb wherever you can. Where it isn't feasible to get a number, work toward it by estimating quantities. Don't use the word, *soon,* if you can reasonably say, *by next week.* And if you're not sure it will be next week, add the word, *probably,* or extend your range another week.

Rather than describing a person as being *oppositional,* it would be much better to say something like, "Most of the time I've asked him to do something, he's fought me on it, putting up one argument or another." Even though the phrase, *most of the time,* is not a precise indication, greater precision isn't necessary in this case; and, *most of the time,* does indicate something over half.

Suppose an executive is given the suggestion: "I don't see any reason for buying from Consolidated since their price is higher than what we're now paying. Even though they give better service, I don't think the difference is worth it." Everything needs to be quantified here. How much higher is the price? What does the service consist of? Does the supplier's salesmen and other representatives visit more often? Are deliveries more often on time ? Does merchandise have to be returned less often because of defects? Is the packaging better? And for all these questions, how much better, how much more often? And still a further question: How much does it matter?

If a supplier has three late shipments out of twenty-five deliveries in a year, even though these three latenesses stick irritatingly in one's mind, the question to be answered is, Can such a record really be beaten considering the great number of influencing factors? And, of course, the degree of lateness on each of these shipments enters in also.

Try to eliminate the subjectivity from the information you give and get. Find out and point out: how much, how often, when, where, as compared to what. And when you get a value, go one step further and ask yourself how significant it is, how much it really matters.

3. THINK IN TERMS OF CONTINUUMS RATHER THAN CATEGORIES (GRAY AREAS RATHER THAN BLACK-OR-WHITE). Annoying though it may be, the truth usually lies somewhere in between. Minds that yearn for tidiness must be continually frustrated by the fact that categories overlap, things are partly true and partly false, and one can't always answer yes or no, or label something as right or wrong.

Although every characteristic of our world exists on a quantity continuum, is present to a certain degree, rather than just either existing or not existing, we tend to think about each characteristic as being there or not there. Something or someone is strong or weak, economical or uneconomical, bright or stupid, honest or dishonest, successful or unsuccessful, or the positive or negative of any other descriptive term. And if one can't assert that a characteristic is present, then it is assumed to be absent.

Instead of describing things as they really are, giving quantities, we try to squeeze them into categories. These categories represent our feeling that there is too little, the right amount, or too much of particular characteristics. There's nothing wrong with categories as long as we realize that reality doesn't come categorized. We classify things into categories of our own making, superimposing on reality the lines demarcating the categories. But categorizing does serve a useful purpose in helping to organize and communicate conceptions.

The trouble is that too often category boundaries are not clearly defined. Everyone operates on his own idea about where categories begin and end—where strong ends and weak begins, where expensive ends and cheap begins, where aggressive ends and timid begins, and where risk ends and certainty begins.

Although each category theoretically represents the whole range of values across that category, that is, a segment of the continuum, it gets to be thought of as a single point. And where there are only two categories, for example, rich and poor, workable and unworkable, the continuum is forgotten. The thinking proceeds as though there were only opposite poles, one for each member of the various pairs of opposing conditions.

For example, a salesman might argue to a buyer for a retail store that he had better buy the salesman's products because they are well advertised and customers will ask for them. The buyer replies that this is no worry to him because he can switch these customers to a brand that he carries. The question that now might form in the salesman's mind is, Can the buyer really switch his customers or can't he?

The buyer's way of expressing his claim that he can switch his customers led the unwary salesman down the path that seemed to offer least resistance—the path of black or white, either-or thinking. Either he can switch his customers or ne can't.

Actually, the whole matter of switching customers exists on

a continuum ranging from switching no customers to switching all customers. And the chances are that the buyer can switch a certain proportion in between. It's as though the opposite poles of this continuum, switch-none and switch-all, are the only parts that exist; and the buyer moves to the nearest pole and expresses himself as though this pole represents the way things really are. Part of this may be motivated by lazy-mindedness, since a pole is easier to think about than a continuum. And part may be motivated by wishful thinking, since he wants to be able to switch them all.

The salesman's move now is to point out the continuum. He might say, "You may be able to switch most of them, but you can't switch them all. What proportion do you think you can switch, eight out of ten?"

The buyer having now to come out from behind his polar thinking (either one pole or the other) will have to face the existence of a certain proportion, no matter how small, that is unswitchable. Pursuing quantifying further, the salesman can then establish with the buyer just how much loss this unswitchable proportion represents in dollars and cents, and quantify still further to estimate the proportion of these customers that would be permanently lost to the store, as well as the loss in traffic.

When you encounter a statement made in terms of something being so or not so, ask yourself if there is anything in between. Can it be partly so and partly not so? For example, if someone says of a new product that advertising will put it over, arguing about whether it will or won't is meaningless. The first questions to ask are, What's meant by putting it over? How much advertising is needed? What is the return per advertising dollar? And is the investment worthwhile? You might then find that the statement is true for a certain amount of advertising and a certain amount of sales but not true for other amounts of these.

Look for gray areas—mixtures of black and white. You'll find that most situations consist of such mixtures. When someone describes something as being a certain way establish in your mind what the opposite is, and then explore for where the true state of things lies along the line between his claim and the opposite.

Generalizations that work are very precious things. They represent the essence of man's knowledge. They are distilled painstakingly drop by drop from the great mass of research.

These precious generalizations enable man to predict and control his environment. Think of some of these magnificent generalizations. When a magnetic field is cut by a wire an electric current flows in the wire. The results: electric power to light up cities, radio and television, motors and generators, and all the vast array of electrical devices.

Those who govern shall do so by consent of the governed. The result: democracy.

When disease germs are injected into the body under certain conditions, the body forms anti-bodies to fight the disease and immunity to that disease is attained. The result: millions of lives saved by innoculation against specific diseases.

And, of course, there are the myriad, useful, lesser generalizations of everyday life. Since generalizations that work are so valuable, is it any wonder that people leap at them, cherishing them even when they are not true? Even if they don't work, until proved wrong they give one an illusion of power.

In the above instance of the buyer, he formed the generalization: When a customer asks for a brand I don't carry, I can switch him to another brand. Holding this illusion gives the buyer a feeling of things being under control. The buyer could have made a more accurate generalization by saying sometning like: When a customer asks for a brand I don't carry, there is a ninety per cent chance that I can switch her to another brand. But this generalization leaves some loose ends, some uncertainty. What about the other ten per cent? So the buyer rejects reality and reaches for the much more alluring kind of generalization—the one that covers every case—and forms it in terms of being able to switch them all.

After all, a generalization with exceptions doesn't provide much security in this uncertain world. The exceptions always loom as a threat. They might sneak in any moment just as one is settling down in the comfort of foreknowledge.

Paradoxically, this hurried generalizing and frantic classifying, in an attempt to establish order in a helter-skelter world, leads to less control rather than more. While knowledge is power, the wrong knowledge leaves one still more helpless than does no knowledge; for with no knowledge, one is prepared to take one's chances, while with wrong knowledge one relaxes, expecting the outcome that doesn't occur, and is unprepared for what materializes.

Recently, a sales executive told me about a company that had its sales force use a canned sales presentation. The salesmen memorized a pre-set sales speech which was to be given to each prospect and covered all the points of the products. This, of course, greatly diminished interaction between salesman and prospect, and eliminated participation by the prospect, and any real drawing out of information, analyzing, and adapting of the presentation by the salesman.

The executive told me that this company had a large sales force, and they found that in using a canned sales presentation, the better salesmen did more poorly than when left to their own devices while the poorer salesmen did better. Balancing the diminished effectiveness of the good salesmen against the increased capability of the poor salesmen, the company found that its sales volume was somewhat higher than before. The executive told me that the conclusion drawn was that a canned sales presentation is more effective than a presentation which allows the salesman to use his own thinking.

At first glance this conclusion might seem warranted and a practical one to make. However, if one considers the situation a little more closely, one realizes that this generalization holds true only if the same standards for selection and development of the salesmen are maintained. But what if the selection procedures were shifted in the direction of hiring salesmen who were more adept at thinking on their feet and developing their own presentations? And what if the training of these salesmen emphasized skill in communicating, in getting ideas through to prospects and motivating them? Then, perhaps, the sales volume would rise again when the salesmen were left to form their own presentations, and the canned sales presentation would fall into disfavor.

4. EVALUATE EACH CASE ON ITS INDIVIDUAL MERITS RATHER THAN PREJUDGING IT FROM GENERALIZATIONS. Making a decision is a trying thing for many people. Choosing one way gives them the feeling that the other way may be better. And for many people the dreadful feeling of being wrong is added to the practical consequences of making the wrong decision. This feeling of having made a mistake is often worse than the results of the mistake, itself.

To avoid the torment of decision-making, people who suffer particularly from the feeling of being wrong resort to the development of all kinds of generalizations to cover as much of their living as possible. Rules are established on when to brush one's teeth, what brands to buy, how to make love to one's mate, what to say to one's children, when to agree with the boss, and any other situations that can somehow be categorized. Instead of deciding about each situation according to its particular characteristics and according to how one feels at the time, one follows rules made to cover all cases, giving up accuracy for security.

The trouble is that situations often don't fit neatly into categories. They often lie on the borderline between categories; and in order to classify them so that a rule can be employed, very meaningful characteristics of a situation are ignored.

Consider company policies, for example. These represent an attempt by top management to cover all situations that are likely to arise in company operation. They are preconceptions based on past experience to cover what *generally* occurs. When applied to the exceptional cases, losses occur. And where there is rigid adherence to policy, losses will be proportionate to the frequency of exceptions.

For example, suppose a company has a policy applying to its

sales force which says that all salesmen must be college graduates. Let's suppose, also, that the sales manager is hard-pressed to find good candidates for his sales positions and that in walks a bright, personable, aggressive individual who very much wants a sales job with the company but has only two years of college. The salesmanager is bound by the policy to reject him. The result is the loss of a very good business-producer for the company.

While it may be true that, on the average, college graduates make better salesmen than non-college graduates, there will be notable exceptions to this. If there were no policy requiring college graduation for a sales position, the sales manager with a high degree of skill in selecting salesmen would create a better sales force, while the sales manager who lacks skill in selecting salesmen would create a poorer one. Basing decisions on averages rather than on the factors in the individual case helps the poorer manager and hinders the skilled one.

In general, policies represent the attempt on management's part to extend their thinking into the field of operations. An attempt is made to anticipate and classify field problems. And then a procedure is given for dealing with them.

This works fairly well if the problems that arise all fall neatly into the established categories. The trouble is that there are too many exceptions. Too often these problems have a way of straddling categories. They don't quite fit into one place or the other and so no procedure or policy adequately covers what to do. Or if it does cover what to do, it often isn't the most productive attack on the problem.

Another source of error is introduced by the fact that the field situation is in a continuous process of change. It takes time for this change to be fed back to top management and fully apprehended by them, and for them to act on it by modifying policies and procedures. As a result, there is always a lag. The company way of dealing with a problem tends to apply to the field situation as it was, rather than as it is.

In clinging to an elaborate set of policies and procedures to govern field operations, top management is in effect saying that even though error is introduced by both an imperfect classification of situations that are likely to arise, and by the time lag in the incorporating of changing conditions, the results are likely to be still more effective than if the field were left to think for itself. Of course, this is not a matter of either one way or the other.

Company policies and procedures are necessary. Management does have certain guide lines it wants followed. And a certain amount of thinking is always left to the field. But the more elaborate the procedures specified, the less management leaves to field thinking, and the more management is wasting one of its most valuable resources—field brains.

Now, losses are incurred by poor thinking in the field. And they are also necessarily incurred by specified procedures that don't fit the field situation closely enough. To minimize the losses, which way is the company to move? Certainly, both policies and independent field thinking are necessary. It's a question of emphasis.

Too often companies are inclined to feel that they have done the best they can with the men in the field and the thing to do is to keep elaborating and specifying further through formalized procedures. And what happens is that the one type of loss—rigid policy, is substituted for another type—poor field thinking, rather than the total loss being diminished.

Why not, instead, focus on improving field thinking? Get men who are potentially better thinkers and develop them still further. Bring them in as much as possible on the aims of top management and train them to examine situations closely, to delve into the implications of their present thinking, to consider various alternative courses of action, and to arrive at the best solutions. And institute controls which require them to check their own thinking.

These men aren't subject to a time lag in getting back field information. Nor do they have to make preconceptions fit what's happening. They can tailor a solution to fit each individual problem. It seems much more productive for top management to select and develop field brains and to use them as initiators and decision-makers rather than merely as executors of preconceived procedures.

In general, try to judge each situation on its individual merits. Whenever you form an opinion take a second look to see if you have really constructed the opinion from the facts in the particular case. Or have you prejudged the case by typing it and referring to some generalization about that type?

For example, are you assuming that a particular man that's fat is jolly; that a particular company is bound by red tape simply because it's big; that a high-placed executive who is a member of the family couldn't have become successful on his own; or that someone is arrogant or lazy or smart or dumb because he is a member of a particular nationality, race, or religion?

Of course, the generalizations of science and of personal experience are valuable in helping you make decisions. But before you use a generalization make sure it is validated by scientific authority or by enough personal experience. And before you apply any generalization, get all the facts available in the particular case. Then see if all these facts still fit into the generalization. If they don't, be wary of how you apply this generalization.

5. CHECK FOR SUPPORTING EVIDENCE WHEN YOU GIVE OR HEAR OPINIONS. Coming to a rational conclusion is complicated by our wishes and feelings. Our feelings are so clever at making a wish look like a fact that we frequently arrive at the conclusion we want rather than at the one that follows from the facts.

Once the desired conclusion has been reached, one doesn't look back to see if the path was lined with facts or home-grown fiction. For example, a male driver in a traffic tangle with a female reasons as follows: It's a woman driver; women drivers are inferior to men drivers; therefore, I'm right and she's wrong

Another example: He's a successful athlete (or movie star) so he must know what he's talking about; therefore, I'll smoke his brand of cigarettes.

In the hiring interview, if the job applicant is good-looking and clean-cut, he generally appears more intelligent, conscientious and reliable than does his more homely rival for the job. In psychology this is called the halo effect. The effect of one trait on the observer spreads to others so that the observer sees in an individual who is desirable in one way, other desirable traits, although there is no evidence for these other traits being present. Similarly, people are quick to believe bad things and slow to accept good, about people they dislike.

How often do we judge the truth of a statement by who made it rather than by the sensibleness of the case for it? If someone makes a statement on some public issue and his political sympathies are very much the same as ours, aren't we so much more willing to give credence to his statement than if his political leanings were alien?

Aren't we always talking about what public personalities are like, the kind of people they are, even though we have never met them? We seem to carry an image of them which actually was formed purely on the basis of information from the press and television. Yet we feel we know them and talk as familiarly about their virtues and vices as though they were everyday friends.

People form all kinds of opinions without bothering with the facts. It's as though the facts were excess baggage and one can travel faster in one's thinking without bothering with them. Certainly, one can jump to conclusions much easier.

Generalizing from a single case is wide-spread and represents wishes leading the mind astray. How often do we hear something like the following:

"Making money in the stock market is just a matter of luck. I know a man who . . ."

"Doctors these days are only interested in making money This lady I know went to this doctor and . . ."

"Education has gone to pot. My son Tommy came home
the other day and . . ."

People too often seem to be guided by generalized images
than by an examination of the facts in the particular case. For
example, an image of salesmen as loud, coarse, joke-telling, ex-
pense-account riding, and uncultured is common. Yet salesmen, like people in other occupations, run the gamut in these
personal traits, so that many salesmen are quite cultivated
people, gracious, considerate, well-read, and even at times a
little reserved.

So many people think of a college campus as a place of
serenity. They don't realize that a place isn't serene. It's people that are or are not serene; and that many professors and
students live with a raging turbulence of emotions within them,
suffering all variations of anxiety, guilt, shame, jealousy, and
varieties of irritability.

Many artists think of business men as phillistines and in-
sensitive boors, although many business men are quite intellectual and artistic in their interests. For example, Crawford
Greenewalt, the president of DuPont, is an eminent authority
on the humming bird, while Wallace Stevens, when a vice
president of an insurance company, was also one of the fore-
most poets in the United States. Businessmen, on the other
hand, often think of artists, writers, and musicians as being
bohemian, non-conformists, living in a world of their own.
Actually, many artists, writers, and musicians live settled family
lives, enjoy sports, and play the stock market.

Many of these images and glib opinions fill an emotional
need. For example, when an individual attacks doctors, education, salesmen, or artists generally, it may represent an outlet
for anger where the real source is hidden. Forming the generalization is like setting up a straw man to attack. Also, many
people feel a little better themselves if they can find others
worse in some way.

When you hear opinions or generalizations, unless they are
based on supporting evidence, discount them as stemming from

feelings or wishes; and before you form a conclusion yourself subject it to the same test.

MAKE THE CONVERSATION OBJECTIVE. In your discussions translate the talk into terms that would form the same conceptions in anybody's mind. For example, a thousand dollars has the same meaning for everyone; but a lot of money is likely to conjure up different images. Define the terms used. Give examples. What is meant precisely by something being efficient or durable, or someone being honest? For efficiency, how much do you get in return for what you put in? For durability, how long does it last and how does this compare with a similar item? And for honesty, how is this impression arrived at?

Watch for tendencies to over-simplify, to move toward one pole or another, black or white, good or bad. For example, someone says, "People won't buy it." What's the evidence for this? Which people does he have in mind? Is it true that all people will react exactly the same way with regard to buying or not buying this particular item? If not, what proportion will buy?

Try to separate your feelings from the reality around you. When you find yourself thinking that you'd really be happy if you had a different job, lived in a different town, had a little more money, or could buy a new home, you may be just avoiding reality. Stop and think for a moment about the continuity of your everyday living. Would any such change really make that much difference in your feelings? When, at some other time in your life, you did have a different job, or a little more money, or lived in a different town, or a different house, were you completely happy then?

Get into the habit of examining each case on its particular merits. Suspend judgment until you've given the case a good scrutiny. Keep feelings and wishes in check for the moment. A way to do this is by asking, What is this based on? How often? How much? What do you mean by this? And do the facts really warrant this conclusion?

As you move toward asking more questions, defining terms,

looking for gray areas instead of just black and white, and waiting with the forming of conclusions until you have the facts, your communication will become clearer and your thinking straighter.

11

Giving and Taking in Conversation

Human relationships thrive on a balance of giving and taking, and generally disintegrate when the flow is too much in one direction. Maintaining a relationship requires that both parties want it. And a loss in the strength of one party's desire is not compensated for by a corresponding gain in the other's desire.

The Flow of Giving and Taking

The relationship is only as strong as the weaker force toward it. The better the balance of giving and taking the more likely is the relationship to flourish and be enjoyed. We all have needs which can be fulfilled only by others. Each seeks fulfillment from another and those that deny others are ultimately in turn rejected.

This giving and taking balance is a very practical matter. One can acquire great material wealth, and experience all kinds of sensual pleasure, solely through taking; but one cannot maintain human relationships without giving. For it is a basic tenet of human behavior that the individual moves in the direction that he expects will lead to personal satisfaction. Unless a relationship is satisfying, it will be discarded.

What do people need from each other? Apart from the material things and favors they exchange, there are affection, approval, encouragement, praise, understanding, sympathy, responsiveness, and an acceptance of one's weaknesses along with respect for one's strengths.

These needs are fulfilled largely through conversation; and even when a particular conversation is not devoted specifically to such fulfillment, these needs will often intrude. If these needs are then not satisfied, the human relationship weakens and perhaps fails at that point, and the other purposes of the conversation are not achieved.

Giving and taking go on continuously in all conversation and the human relationship is sustained by this reciprocal flow. If the flow becomes onesided, the relationship wanes for the moment. The conversational fire burns low and dies out. There is no more fuel to feed the occasional spark of interest that flares momentarily.

The word, *giving,* is used here in a sense of giving up some thing for the benefit of another person. It does not merely refer to the direction of interchange. For example, someone may give another person a blow or an insult. One may give orders, or give a paper to sign, or an object to examine. In that sense the word, *give,* is used to represent merely the direction of the action.

However, giving for the benefit of another, generally involves giving up energy, time, or things in order to fulfill the other person's needs and desires. As such, the very act of giving implies an awareness of the other person as being human like one's self, rather than merely an object to be acted on and taken from. Giving represents to some extent an identification with the interests of the other person. This makes giving an act of love. Of course, all gifts are not necessarily given out of love. But because it is reminiscent of loving it kindles responsiveness.

Most people have needs, appetites, and desires that are constantly pressing for fulfillment. As a result, there are always opportunities for giving. For example, there are so many things people want to learn about where one could give knowledge. Also people want to bolster their image of themselves. They want to feel that they are bright, good looking, kindly, rational, and generally worthy members of mankind. Very often they look to another person to give them reassurance as though the other person were a mirror through which they could evaluate their acceptability.

People need outlets for their feelings. They need someone who will listen with understanding; who will give them reassurance for their anxiety, a vent for their anger, acceptance and forgiveness for their guilt, sympathy for their grief and who will share their joy.

This ever-present desire for information, attention, reassurance, comfort, and sympathy, calls for a great deal of giving. And this kind of giving is done almost entirely in conversation.

While the giving of material things and the doing of favors are more obvious forms of giving and are likely to cost more money, giving in conversation is much more frequent, more subtle, and though of little material value, often much more appreciated. Conversational giving is generally the mortar that holds together warm, productive human relationships.

Although conversational giving generally costs little money it may involve something still more precious—one's attention, concern, interest, sympathy, and resourcefulness. And it generally satisfies deeper hungers than those for material things.

In conversation, giving and taking can be done both when one is talking and when one is listening. Let's discuss now each of these four ways in turn: giving through talking, giving through listening, taking through talking, and taking through listening.

Giving Through Talking

Three ways in which you can give through talking are: (1) educating; (2) entertaining; and (3) fulfilling emotional needs. Educating is used broadly here to include the giving of any facts or information, criticizing constructively, sharing of one's personal experiences, and the giving of helpful advice and suggestions.

Entertaining includes the telling of jokes or amusing or exciting stories, and stimulating through riddles or puzzles.

You are fulfilling emotional needs while talking when you praise, reassure, sympathize, or take notice in some way of something the other person might be proud of.

Sometimes these different ways occur simultaneously. For example, when you share your personal feelings with someone not only are you giving him information about your reactions but you are also implying your confidence in him by your willingness to reveal yourself. Similarly, when you tell a funny story not only are you giving pleasure directly but you are also subtly indicating that you care enough about the other person to give your time and effort to amuse him.

In a conversation between a doctor and his patient the doctor gives through talking when he explains the nature of the illness, when he gives instructions, when he gives reassurance to allay anxiety, and when he tells the patient what to expect or how well other patients progressed with the same ailment.

A supervisor gives to his subordinate through talking when he gives information and instructions for performing the job, when he praises the subordinate, when he gives constructive suggestions, when he informs the subordinate about how well he is doing, and when he tells the subordinate of the possibili ties that lie ahead.

Through his words the supervisor also gives reassurance when the subordinate is anxious, sympathy when the subordinate is depressed, and expressions of appreciation, and congratulations, and a general sharing of joy when good things happen to the subordinate. And all these things that the supervisor gives through talking are given also by the teacher to his pupil, by the parent to his child, and by the clergyman to his church members.

The salesman gives through talking when he provides information useful to the prospect either in his business or for his personal life. For example, the salesman might suggest helpful methods of selling or using merchandise, or of running a business generally, that the salesman might have learned from other similar businesses. Or he might give interesting facts about the prospect's hobbies. The salesman might give helpful advice, tell an amusing story, praise the prospect, or reassure the prospect on some trouble he has.

The salesman's talk is conversational giving when it is done for the benefit of the prospect. Even if the salesman hopes to gain eventually from it, this doesn't prevent it from being giving. The fact is that the prospect is gaining at the moment from the salesman's talking.

Words then can be gifts. They can reward with pleasure as real as that resulting from tangible gifts. Often, they are received with much greater satisfaction.

Giving Through Listening

To someone in need of an outlet for his thoughts and feelings, your attention can be a precious gift. As a listener you are more than a recipient of information. You are often an instrument for both the crystallization of thoughts, and the discharge of feelings. Let's consider each of these.

HELPING THOUGHTS CRYSTALLIZE. Thinking is a rather disorderly process. Ideas form in the mind under the pressure of a variety of competing needs within the individual. And associations are made with other ideas that are related in some way in the individual's mind. These follow each other in a helter-skelter way as the needs press and the associations occur, without regard for what is relevant to the immediate line of reasoning.

It's as though there were a crowd of ideas all assembled around the circle of awareness and all pressing to get into this circle, into the spotlight of consciousness. The ones with more force behind them make it through even though they are not logically relevant.

This procession of ideas on the stage of the mind are expressions of feelings that are pressing for discharge. Often they are unproductive fantasies. Still, in some personal sense they are satisfying to the individual even though they may not represent the accomplishment of some immediate goal. Daydreaming does bring pleasure and releases a certain amount of tension, even though it isn't constructive.

At the same time the individual has his immediate goals to accomplish which require orderly thinking. He has to think through the problems he faces and keep out distracting tangential thoughts. Sometimes it is too difficult to resist the pressures of these fantasies and as a result little productive thinking is done.

The individual repeatedly starts toward his goal only to be drawn away by some seductive inner Circe calling to him. His self-discipline isn't quite strong enough at the moment to keep him along the narrow path of productive thinking, and he succumbs and wanders afield.

The presence of a listener often serves to support the individual's struggle to direct his thinking toward his goal. In order to communicate with the listener the individual has to put his thoughts into understandable language. And in order to do this he has to screen out those ideas that are irrelevant and place the relevant ideas in an orderly sequence that leads to some conclusion. The act of verbalizing is a great help in pulling thoughts together. In the privacy of one's fantasies one doesn't have to make sense. But to communicate effectively, and to make a good impression, and to be convincing, good sense is needed.

As a listener, therefore, you stimulate the individual to search in his mind for useful material and to organize this material so that it moves toward an objective. And many people need the stimulus of an audience in order to get out their ideas clearly. The listener acts as a sounding board. The individual can try his ideas on the listener and then step back to see how they look. Helping the other person to think out his thoughts by your attentive listening will encourage him to reciprocate by listening to your ideas, as a way of showing his appreciation.

HELPING TO DISCHARGE FEELINGS. In conversation, the listener frequently acts as a vehicle for the discharge of feelings by the speaker. An individual who is annoyed or worried or joyful or guilty about something has to carry the burden of these pent up feelings until he can vent them. Probably the most common way of venting feelings is talking. And talking calls for a listener.

Of course, people often talk to themselves under the pressure of their feelings. For example, I heard a typist in the outer office muttering to herself. She had had her lunch sent up to the office and on opening it she exclaimed in exasperation, "I ordered a roast beef and tomato and they sent me a ham and cheese." There was no one in the office with her but the feeling of frustration was great enough to require vocalization.

The scream of pain, the sob of despair, the moan of grief, the gasp of surprise, the cry of delight, and the peal of laughter are all vocalizations of intense emotion. No listener is required here. The force of the feeling is great enough to trigger these expressions.

But there is a whole variety of feelings of lesser intensity that press for discharge. Still, they are not strong enough to erupt by themselves. A listener is needed to complete the circuit.

This steady current of feeling—whether anxiety, joy, anger, shame, jealousy, embarrassment, and any combination of these —prods the individual gently but insistently to find an outlet, to somehow work an expression of them into the conversation.

These feelings are not sharp enough to require immediate vocalization so talking to one's self or crying out are unnecessary. One can hold on to these feelings and wait until a listener is available so that the possibility of getting sympathy, reassurance, or praise greatly adds to the relief of discharge.

An executive recently told me of his annoyance with his wife's tendency to anticipate what he intends to say, and to finish his sentences for him. She simply doesn't realize that conversation plays much more of a role than the transmission of ideas from one mind to another. It serves as a discharge for feelings as well, and she kept monopolizing the discharge, while her husband's feelings remained bottled up.

Keep in mind, therefore, that in listening you are contributing comfort to another individual. You are enabling him to discharge tension, to talk out his feelings. While you may not be gaining any useful information, the time you are giving is contributing to the cultivation of the relationship. Somewhere inside him he recognizes that you have given up your time and attention to make him more comfortable. And he is likely to appreciate this and value your company for it.

Taking Through Talking

Taking through talking is the reverse of giving through listening. When you talk to release pent up feelings you are using the time and attention of your listener to make yourself more comfortable. He generally gains nothing. Or if he does gain, it is not because of any intention on your part.

When you use another person as an instrument for the discharge of your feelings there is a certain amount of giving in this also. You are giving him the compliment of sharing your feelings with him, of making him your confidant. You are implying that you trust him enough to reveal yourself to him.

But when the discharge continues until the demand on his time becomes excessive the giving aspect is lost in the imposition. And when one is experiencing the pleasure of ventilating his feelings time can go very quickly. Furthermore, the speaker, in finding the conversation so satisfying to him because of this discharge, may assume that it is equally satisfying to his listener.

This illusion that one's own joy is necessarily experienced by others is demonstrated in a conversation related to me recently. A woman, on encountering a friend, remarked that she had good news for the friend. The friend's face lit up with eager anticipation, only to hear the speaker remark that she herself had been able to get the maid that she wanted for the summer. The woman receiving this piece of news remarked to me that she was appalled at the insensitivity of this woman, who described her own securing of a desired maid as good news for the friend.

While time flits for you it may drag for your listener. Your feelings are being pleasantly released. His are being held in. While he started off with sympathy and the pleasure of being your chosen repository of personal feelings, his pleasure begins to wear thin and he becomes impatient to pursue his own business.

Therefore, as soon as the clouds of feeling that dim your perspective abate enough to enable you to catch your first clear sight of your listener as an individual, rather than as just an ear, bring him into the conversation. Ask for his reactions. Give him a chance to sound off.

Taking Through Listening

Taking through listening is the reverse of giving through talking. When you listen to information, praise, advice, reassurance, and encouragement you are taking in either useful ideas or ones that contribute good feelings. And while the speaker may be flattered by your attentiveness he is likely to become irritated after awhile if you give him nothing back in return.

While having a good listener has its charms for the speaker, he finds this pleasure palling when he begins to feel drained. If the listener draws out of the speaker all the pertinent useful information, elicits from the speaker praise and reassurance as well, and then gives nothing back in return, the speaker is likely to feel used, merely a source to be sucked dry.

Attentive listening is considered a prime way of cultivating the good will of others. This needs to be qualified. Attentive listening has its charm only when it serves as an outlet for the other person. But when it serves only the listener it can be quite wearing on the speaker.

You can be a very attentive listener while conducting a cross-examination. You keep making demands for information while he keeps fulfilling them. This certainly produces anything but friendly feeling in the cross-examinee.

Whether you are receiving useful information or praise or reassurance, express your appreciation of it. Indicate how helpful it is, or how glad you are to hear it. If you have anything worthwhile to give back this is a good place to do it. Even if the situation were set up purposely for you to take through listening, try to get a little flow going back in the other direction.

Share The Talking Time

A conversation contains within it potential treasure for both parties. A span of human time and attention is quite an asset, and both parties to the conversation are pooling their time and attention. Add to time and attention a measure of information and a capacity for giving praise and reassurance and one can readily see that there are prized resources to be had from this conversational pool. And by the end of the conversation each will have taken out a certain proportion. The question remains, How much will each get?

Sometimes there is mutual cooperation. Each takes out a fair share. At other times one may take out much more than another and yet the division is satisfying to both sides since one may want to give to and help the other.

However, at other times there may be sharp competition for these riches with each attempting to control the conversation in order to exploit it more fully. There may be competition over who is going to use the available time to vent his troubles. There may be vying with each other for the other's sympathy. Each may be seeking praise. And one may want to use the conversation to get information from the other while the other may need it to discharge some pent up feelings.

This struggle for control of the conversation may take the form of interrupting, steering the conversation, changing the subject, answering a question with a question, or just plain occupying of the time through long speeches.

Competing for the use of the conversation has an alienating effect. When each person in the conversation struggles agains the other to use the conversation for his own purposes each inevitably feels frustrated by the other. Since each wants it all and neither can have the whole thing, both are bound to feel deprived.

The ironic thing is that since both are struggling for the same thing, each is too tense, because of his own avid grasping, to listen attentively to the other. As a result all that each gets is the time to talk, but not the attention of the other person. Each is merely waiting for his turn until he can blurt out what is on his mind.

It's futile to engage in this kind of competition. If you have to struggle for another person's attention in the face of his struggling for yours, even if you win the struggle, you are not likely to gain much. The struggle itself tends to destroy responsiveness.

It would be much more productive for you to start your conversations with the idea that you are going to give up part of them to the other person's needs. Keep in mind that your own ends will be much better served by having your conversational partner share in the conversation.

At times you may have the feeling that you have too much to cover and there isn't enough time. This doesn't matter. If you persist in monopolizing the conversation you'll be the only one covering your material. Your listener will have tuned out. And he is likely to be resentful as well.

Giving And Taking Are Habits Characteristic Of The Individual

Many people characteristically enjoy giving while others give largely because they expect some reward in return or because they realize that a certain amount of giving is necessary to get along with others.

In conversation then, those who enjoy giving are likely to do it without deliberation, while those who take no pleasure from giving do so out of necessity, to encouraging cooperation on the part cf the other person.

Since giving and taking are characteristic reactions of the individual, rather than being specifically directed toward particular people, there is no point in your being offended by someone who keeps trying to take from you in a conversation. He has not picked you out to exploit. He is not directing his conversational greed at you particularly. This is characteristic of him, and he may even like you and enjoy your company and still feel compelled by habit to take as much as he can from the conversation, just as he does from other activities.

Similarly, you should not necessarily feel especially flattered at being the recipient of someone else's sympathy or information. This individual may be a characteristic giver, enjoying contributing to others; and here again you are not being singled out as the target of his affection. He just enjoys giving and you happen at the moment to be in interaction with him.

Of course, a certain amount of discrimination takes place too so that individuals may give more to certain preferred persons than to others. Similarly, the taker may curb his taking somewhat, out of affection for a particular individual. But it is likely that both forces are operating here: the attitude toward the particular individual and the tendency toward giving and taking.

Giving Is Necessary To Communicate Persuasively

A fundamental principle in good communicating is that the listener's receptivity must be established and maintained. A great deal of conversation is lost simply because receptivity is taken for granted. It's assumed that silence implies listening. Even though people know this isn't so, they seem to act as though it were when addressing others.

Also, people seem to have a misplaced faith in their ability to gauge other peoples attentiveness from the expression on their face. This is impossible to do. Wide-eyed expressions of rapt absorption, rhythmic nodding, and intermittent vocalizing of "uh-huh" can be presented to the speaker while the listener mentally resides in his own far-away fantasy.

People are so wrapped up in what to say and how to say it that they ignore the crucial problem of how to get the other person to listen. A prime attention-distractor is the individual's own need to speak. This need to speak may arise from several sources. He may want to question what you say because he doubts it or disagrees with it. He may not have comprehended clearly what you are getting at and wants you to clarify it. He may want to affirm what you say out of some need to show that he is in agreement with you. Or he may want to talk about something else that is on his mind.

But whatever the force, the urge to speak interferes with his focusing on what you are saying. Furthermore, if he fails to comprehend something, he's likely to tune out on what follows since he has lost his orientation. And if he disagrees, he may concentrate on building his case for disagreement rather than listening to what follows; or he may abandon attentiveness because he feels that what follows may be as wrong as what he has just heard, and therefore not worth listening to.

To minimize these distractors you have to find outlets for the other person's urge to speak. If he doesn't take the initiative himself you should draw him out at points along the way to make sure that he is not inhibiting this urge. Even if inhibited, it interferes. If the other person has things on his mind he wants to talk about, you have to allow time for it even though it is unrelated to the subject you want to discuss.

This does not mean that on all occasions you are to devote as much time as the other person wants for airing his problems. Other demands on your time should be taken into consideration. For example, a salesman who has a certain number of calls to make for the day can't allow unlimited time for a buyer to emotionally ventilate. But some time has to be given to this, whether it's ten or twenty minutes or whatever can be spared. Even if it's time taken away from a sales presentation, this time is not wasted. It helps to cultivate the relationship since the buyer is aware that time is being given up for his sake.

Similarly, managers have to allow time for subordinates to complain angrily, express their worries, and talk out their ideas generally. It isn't enough for a manager, when confronted by a subordinate who is angry or bitter about some real or imagined mistreatment, to tell the subordinate to think it over, write out his position, and then come back. The subordinate wants to let out his feelings and he needs a listener, and the manager should take this role. Again, it stands to reason that the manager can't do this endlessly; but a certain amount of his time should be devoted to it if he expects to have good relationships with subordinates.

No matter what kind of activity you are engaged in and no matter how much efficiency you are striving for, you still have to recognize that people operate on both an idea level and a feeling level and both of these must be dealt with.

You can't respond only to what passes your test of logic. You have to also show the other person that you care about how he feels. Feelings have a way of distorting thinking so that what seems illogical to you may be logical to him and the other way around, as well. Logical or not, ideas represent a striving for a solution to a felt problem and must be given consideration if the relationship is to flower.

Cultivate the habit of giving time to the other person's talking out his ideas and discharging his feelings. Not only are your relationships likely to be much better but a lot more of what you say will get through.

12

Getting Through to Groups

Reaching minds when talking to groups calls for essentially the same techniques as are needed for successful conversation between two people. Such barriers to communication as distracting inner preoccupations, emotions pressing for release, preconceptions that conflict with the ideas being presented, the listener's tuning out because he thinks he knows what the speaker is going to say, the limiting rate at which information can be assimilated, and other interferences discussed earlier in this book apply to group communication as well as to two-party conversation.

However, the group situation poses some additional difficulties.

Six Obstacles To Getting Ideas Through To Groups

1. VARYING INTERESTS. The remarks of the speaker must be pitched to the group as a whole. In talking to one person you

can frame your ideas and adjust your language to best capture the interests of the other person. You can tie in your ideas with the other person's needs. In the group you can only appeal to those needs they have in common and you can only use organization and content that will best get through to all. Often, these common elements are much less effective for getting through than certain specifics would be for certain individuals. But these specifics don't apply to all, and while using them would attract some it would alienate others.

2. WITHDRAWN ATTENTION. One feels easier about withdrawing his attention from the speaker in a group than in a two-party conversation. He reasons that if he misses anything he can always get it from others who are there. Also, there are always plenty of other people to respond to anything the leader asks the group. He doesn't have the responsibility of being a conversational partner. He is merely one of an audience. There is less force holding him to the talk, to counter-balance any inner motivation to mentally withdraw.

3. IRRELEVANCE. When individual group members, by comments or questions to the speaker, use this opportunity to unburden themselves of problems that bear little relevance to the topic under discussion, others will lose interest and mentally depart.

4. LESS PARTICIPATION. There is less opportunity to get feedback from group members. Certainly, some of this can and should be done but it can't possibly be as extensive as it is in conversation between two people. As a result, group members won't be making the ideas presented part of their thinking to as great an extent as is done in conversation between two people. In the group there is relatively too much passive listening. Since the listener isn't prodded to articulate in his own words the ideas presented to him, much of it will merely be heard and then evaporate from the surface of his mind. He hasn't really worked on it enough to absorb and retain it.

5. SUPPRESSED EMOTION. The more limited opportunity for feedback by listeners necessarily requires greater containment of their emotional pressures. Although emotions that are pressing for release create a kind of static, distracting them from

listening, they have to bear with this in the group situation and as a result there is bound to be a certain loss in absorption of ideas.

6. MAGNIFIED INHIBITIONS AND IMPULSES. The group mem- bers' personality needs and fears that generally tend to inhibit expression are magnified in the group situation. The fear of saying the wrong thing would be greater when there are a number of people who might hear it instead of only one. The temptation to impress others is similarly enlarged when there are more people to be impressed, so that remarks are often made for this purpose rather than to further understanding. And any desire to attack authority, apart from the issues, is much more likely to be expressed where support can be mobilized.

And while the obstacles to getting through are greater in the group situation than in two-party conversation, the op- portunities for dealing with these obstacles are less. Therefore, communication is bound to be less efficient in the group, and one should not expect to communicate as much to several minds simultaneously as to one mind. Whether a meeting is held as a training class, or as a session for imparting new views or direc- tives, or as a conference to set forth objectives and methods for achieving them, keep in mind the communication limits. Set- ting your goals realistically will prevent later chagrin over ideas that were never absorbed.

Still, there are techniques that can be used to step up com- munication to the group. These are essentially the techniques that apply to face-to-face communication but need to be modi- fied to fit the group situation.

Three Techniques For Getting
Your Ideas Through To Groups

1. Orient the group's thinking. Start your talk by pointing the minds of your audience toward your objective. Let them know what you're getting at. In effect, tell them what you're going to tell them.

Too often speakers seem afraid to plunge right in. They give reasons for the point they want to make before making it and as a result the audience has no frame of reference for these reasons. Or the speaker talks first about a problem, with no preliminary indication of whether he has a solution to it, or in what direction this solution lies. The audience is never quite sure of whether the speaker is complaining about a bothersome situation, is asking for help, or means to propose some action.

Sometimes, a speaker may feel timid about setting forth an idea unless he has first given all the foundation for this idea. There is nothing wrong with giving foundations as long as the audience knows what they're for. But when they're given first —perhaps because the speaker feels anxious about the audience challenging his idea unless he gives its proof first—the audience is likely to feel a little frustrated at not knowing what the speaker is leading up to.

As an example, if you've called a meeting to tell the group about a new procedure that's to be instituted, don't start off by telling about all the problems and difficulties that make the new procedure necessary. First, tell what the new procedure is and then give the justification for it. What you're talking about should come before why you're talking about it.

2. **Give examples.** Whenever you deal with groups of people you might just as well operate on the basic premise that whenever multiple interpretations are possible, they will be made. Therefore, when you set forth an idea that might be subject to various interpretations, give an example. Illustrate its application through a specific case.

The more you, as the speaker, are used to your own interpretation, the more likely are you to be unaware of other possible interpretations. You'll be taking for granted that your audience knows what you mean. And each member of the audience will similarly take for granted that he understands you rightly, even though the various members of the audience may unknowingly have varying interpretations.

Whenever you're dealing with groups you can rely on the laws of chance providing a distribution of reactions and interpretations among the group. And the larger the group the more you can depend on this happening. Whenever I taught fairly large classes and gave an examination I could rely on several examination papers coming in without bearing the student's name.

Giving examples will minimize multiple interpretation. For example, if you're asking a group to show more initiative, or to limit expenditures to what's absolutely necessary, or if you tell them that team spirit is lacking, or that standards have slipped, give an example. Of course, if what you're saying is absolutely definite, not at all subject to interpretation, you don't need the example. And a good way to decide this is to follow the rule: Unless a specific quantity, or a specific point in space or time is mentioned, an example is necessary.

If you refer to a meeting that will take place in Philadelphia at nine o'clock on October 10 you don't need an example. The points of space and time are specified. But if you say that everybody is expected to be at the meeting unless something extremely urgent arises to prevent their attendance, you had better give an example of something extremely urgent, to help define what you mean.

3. **Provide for feedback.** In order to get the members of your group to grasp your ideas firmly it is essential that they perform some mental work on these ideas. Since you can't depend on their initiating such mental activity you have to prod them in order to elicit feedback.

The term feedback is a little misleading here since it puts the emphasis on getting back information on what your audience is thinking. Actually the main purpose of the feedback is not so much to find out what's on their minds as to make them think. The very process of feeding back requires that they think about what you are saying.

Three Ways To Provide For Feedback

A. ASK QUESTIONS. Questions are excellent thought-prodders. In the course of the talk you are giving, intersperse questions frequently. You might even make it a rule that you not talk for more than thirty seconds without asking a question. These questions can be of two types: those you wait for the group to answer; and those you answer yourself.

Those which involve the group in answering are more thought-stimulating but there are times when they can't be used perhaps because the audience is too large or because you don't want to spare the time for group discussion. Still, questions are needed to keep the minds of the audience in motion. And the question that you answer yourself, or that you leave unanswered because its answer is quite evident from what you are saying, is still a very good thought-activator.

People are conditioned to start thinking when asked a question. They are habituated to start organizing a response to the question, and in order to do this their minds must go into action. Therefore, if you pose a question to the audience and pause for a moment, the wheels will start to turn out of sheer habit. Then, even if you answer the question yourself you have jogged them into reaching for the answer.

The asking of questions need not be confined to the talk itself. Questions can precede the talk to sound out the thinking of the group and to alert their minds to the answers that are coming in the talk. For example, in my sessions in persuasive communication, the first part is a quiz where the group has to select answers for twelve multiple-choice questions.

I then give a talk during which the group is free to interrupt me with any questions they have. After the talk the same quiz is given and they are asked to again select answers. Thinking through these same questions after listening to the talk serves to crystallize in their minds the ideas presented. Following this there is discussion of the questions and their answers, and this serves to further entrench these ideas. This method could be used for almost any group meeting. Simply prepare a set of questions to be answered by the group both before and after the talk, and then discussed.

When you plan your talk include questions as part of the plan. And work out these questions as carefully as you do the ideas you intend to present. Not only will your audience learn much more about what you're saying but they'll enjoy the talk more. It'll draw them closer to you since they'll be thinking along with you. And they'll have the pleasure of mental exercise.

B. ENCOURAGE QUESTIONS. A question is a reaching for information or for mental contact or both. When members of the group ask questions it's a sign of their interest and of their actively trying to make the ideas they're receiving a part of their thinking. When you give a talk you ought to do more than welcome questions. You should actively encourage them.

The first question seems to be the hardest to get someone to ask. Probably everyone is unsure of just how the question will be received and is a little anxious therefore about what position he will be placed in by asking it.

Three ways to encourage questions from the group

(a) Let the group know that questions will be gladly received. And I favor having the group interrupt me with any questions they have as they come to mind rather than waiting until the talk is finished. When a question is hot in a person's mind he is much more receptive to the answer. By the end of the talk he may have forgotten or lost interest in what he was going to ask. Also, people can't mentally hold on to all the things that come to mind during the talk. Therefore only part of the questions that bother them will be brought up. And asking them to write down their questions doesn't work very well since many people in the group won't be sufficiently motivated to go to the trouble. And those that do write their questions, won't care as much by the end of the talk, for other concerns will have crowded into their minds.

(b) Plan for a place in your talk, preferably near the beginning, where you can stop and ask the group something like.

"What would be the sensible question to ask at this point?" You should set up your opening material so that it leads to a natural question. Once someone raises his hand and asks a question it will be much easier for others to follow suit.

(c) Praise questions when they're given. If a group member is rewarded by having his question praised as being interesting, astute, penetrating, thought-provoking, and one that makes the speaker glad it was asked, other group members will be encouraged to seek similar praise by asking questions.

Another, more subtle, way of praising a question is by asking others how they would answer it. Doing this implies that the question is worthy of more extensive thought and comment than is provided merely by your own answer. This method can be used together with the more direct praise of the question.

C. PROBE QUESTIONS FROM THE AUDIENCE. When a question is asked, rather than answering it immediately, draw it out. Ask the person to elaborate a little on his question. You might also summarize back to him your understanding of his question and then ask him if this is what he means. This assumes of course that the question isn't merely one of simple fact.

If his question is at all subject to more than one interpretation and you interpret it other than the way he means it, your answer will be unsatisfying, and he will be frustrated and a little alienated. Furthermore, others in the group who chose his interpretation will similarly feel that you don't appreciate their thinking or don't clearly understand the problem, yourself. Another way of making sure is by asking the questioner whether your answer is satisfactory. This gives you another opportunity to give him what he wants in case your answer isn't adequate. And if you don't ask him, he may be dissatisfied and not reveal it.

It's essential in planning a talk that you provide a time allowance for feedback. Therefore, when trying to decide how many items you can cover in the time allotted, remember the time you have is the total time minus the feedback time. If you succumb to the temptation to squeeze in some more items by eliminating the feedback, you'll lose the whole talk.

Allow For A Certain Amount Of Irrelevancy

During the meeting, ideas will be brought up that are only remotely connected to the topic at hand. The various group members will be travelling mentally along their individual paths of associated ideas, and each of these paths will be different. Many of these group members will keep their associated thoughts to themselves realizing that they have no immediate relevancy. Others will feel the need to vocalize their ideas.

A certain amount of such irrelevant discussion should be allowed. Many conference leaders clamp down too severely on such irrelevancy, some because they pride themselves on their ability to differentiate between the relevant and irrelevant and feel that they want to run a highly efficient meeting; and others because they are afraid the meeting will get out of hand if they allow any digression whatever.

Both of these illusions diminish the effectiveness of a meeting. If all irrelevancy is stifled the suppressed pressure behind the irrelevant ideas will distract the individual from absorbing the ideas the speaker is trying to get across. Not only is the frustrated person's receiving channel likely to be blocked but his frustration may lead him to oppose the ideas being presented just to get even. Furthermore others may become reluctant to ask questions or comment for fear of their ideas being considered irrelevant.

As for the meeting getting out of hand, this is an unwarranted anxiety. The speaker always has control. He can always terminate the digression at whatever point he wishes. Keep this in mind when you lead a meeting so that you allow for a certain amount of irrelevant discussion.

Repeat As You Go Along
And Summarize At the End

Human limitations in the absorption of ideas make it impossible for your whole talk to be grasped as a result of a single exposure. In fact, it's likely that only a small part of it will be really digested. Just as anything is progre. ively learned as a result of repetition, the more times your ideas are repeated the more of it will be implanted. This means that you have to provide repetition within your talk and at the same time not be monotonous.

As you go through your talk keep spiraling back to previous ideas but present them in a new context or new application. This new association will eliminate monotony and at the same time provide repetition. For example, presenting an idea to the group and then telling how you arrived at the idea is an interesting way of enabling you to repeat that idea several times. Then, telling about your experience with the idea repeats the idea again. And telling what others think of the idea is a third way of repeating. And relating this idea to another idea mentioned earlier in your talk not only repeats this idea in a fourth way but provides another repetition of the earlier idea.

When you plan your presentation to the group prepare in advance ways of repeating the ideas you intend to present. And the more complex the idea, or the more ideas being presented, the more often repetition will be required.

This means that your allotted time for the items you want to present will be reduced not only by the time required for feedback but that required for repetition. Be sure you do your subtracting first and then prepare only as many items as you can present in the remaining time. And be sure to prepare and leave time for a summary at the end. This provides another repetition. Without feedback, repetition, and summarizing you'll be the only one covering the material. Your audience will be left behind.

Providing for feedback and repetition may seem bothersome and time-consuming but human thinking and learning being what it is, there is no other way. Getting ideas to take root is a painstaking process. It requires that the speaker not only present ideas clearly, but that he make the audience grasp them.

13

Persuading

Persuading Means Implanting
A New Way of Reacting

Thoughts, feelings, and actions are responses to stimuli that come from two sources: the world around us; and our inner world.

Although there are many things happening in both outer and inner worlds, we can't respond to everything at the same time; so we try to do those things that will best deal simultaneously with external and internal events.

For example, suppose a salesman is interviewing a prospect The prospect is stimulated from without by the appearance and manner of the salesman, and by the information presented. The prospect's inner stimuli come from irritations, wishes, and worries, and from the demands of other tasks that need to be done. The prospect's feelings about the salesman as a person, and about being influenced, also become internal stimuli affecting his responses.

The prospect reacts not merely to the salesman's presentation but to a complex of events that include the salesman and his presentation among others. In effect, the prospect's response will be a composite of reactions to all these occurrences both around and within him.

Similarly, the salesman's response is a product of outer and inner events. Some possible forces within him are: anxiety over being rejected by the prospect or criticized by his own boss; impatience to get what he wants; lack of confidence in his product or in his selling prowess; and resentment toward the prospect for not being more friendly or for having kept him waiting.

The external factors acting on the salesman might include: the appearance and attitude of the prospect; his reactions toward the salesman and toward his product; and the size and decor of the prospect's office. If, for example, these frighten the salesman, he may talk too fast, or interrupt the prospect, or withdraw too easily in the face of resistance, or avoid asking for an order, or neglect to draw out the prospect's needs.

Although all these things are happening simultaneously in any given conversation, the person speaking tends to adopt the illusion that he is the only thing that is happening to the listener at the moment. This in turn leads the speaker to believe that what he says and does are the only things determining how the other person reacts. If the listener reacts angrily or joyfully or anxiously, the speaker feels that he caused it.

Now in order to persuade the prospect to buy his product the salesman has to change a particular reaction of the prospect. The salesman has to get the prospect to respond by buying the salesman's product rather than a competitive one. And this implanting of the new response in place of the old, has to be done in the face of all the other distracting but simultaneously occurring events.

While selling is one use of persuasion, if we view persuasion as getting another person to adopt a different reaction from one previously given, we can readily see that persuasion covers a whole gamut of activities.

Much of Purposeful Conversation Is Persuasion

Viewing persuasion as the instilling and strengthening of responses in others, we can see that we are frequently engaged in persuading. Often, we try to induce in others a response of admiration or respect or delight when they encounter us. We want them to think well of us. Implanting such a response is a form of persuading.

The parent persuades the child to adopt desired behavior patterns; the doctor persuades the patient to respond to illness by following a prescribed course of medication; the lawyer persuades the jury; the manager persuades his subordinates; and lovers persuade each other. Whenever we try to get someone to think, feel, or do something that he might not otherwise do, we are persuading.

Four Rules For Persuading

1. RECEPTIVITY MUST BE ESTABLISHED. Unless a person is in a state of readiness to receive a particular idea, he isn't likely to accept it. This state of readiness hinges on three factors:

   (a) Freedom from distraction by inner preoccupations.
   (b) The relationship between this new idea and the ideas he already holds. If accepting this new idea would require too much of a reshuffling and discarding of existing notions, he is likely to be unreceptive.
   (c) The effect that the new idea has on his self-image. If the new idea is a blow to his ego he is likely to reject it.

Often, the second and third factors above are related to each other in that a man may do the second—hold to a conception which is false—because it helps him to accomplish the third—sustain the self-image he wants. For example, a man who greedily devotes his energies to getting as much as he can may hold the conception that everybody is this way. This conception makes him feel less greedy since by comparison he is then not greedy at all.

2. QUESTIONS AND EXPRESSIONS OF DOUBT INDICATE RECEP-
TIVITY. How can we tell when a person is in a state of receptivity? Receptivity is indicated by the asking of a question or
any other expression of wanting to know more, or by expressions of self-doubt. Such expressions reflect a gap or vacuum
that is waiting to be filled. And the other person then is receptive to ideas that will fill this vacuum.

On the other hand, when an individual makes a definite assertion he isn't likely to be receptive to anything that in any way
conflicts with this assertion. A statement that ends with a period
points to less receptivity than one that ends with a question
mark. The firmer or more positive the declaration, the nar-
rower is the receiving channel.

Here are some examples of higher and lower receptivity
statements:

Prospect to Salesman
>Lower receptivity: "Your price is too high."
>Higher receptivity: "Why should I pay your price when
>I can get it for ten per cent less
>elsewhere?"

Child to Parent
>Lower receptivity: "I would have gotten a higher
>mark but the teacher has it in for
>me."
>Higher receptivity: "I don't know where I fell down in
>this subject."

Subordinate to Superior
>Lower receptivity: "This procedure doesn't make sense,
>considering all the trouble you
>have to go through."
>Higher receptivity: "I wish I could see the purpose of
>this procedure, considering all the
>trouble involved."

Student to Teacher
>Lower receptivity: "I know the answer but I just can't
>put it into words."

Higher receptivity: "I wonder why I have so much difficulty answering this question."

Of course, one has to note the tone of voice, as well, in determining receptivity. A question asked in a belligerent manner
may reflect less receptivity than a statement made in a reflective
way. The comment, given in an angry tone, "Why the devil
didn't you tell me before moving ahead?" is not a request for
information, despite its interrogatory form, but an angry attack.

3. HOLD YOUR ARGUMENTS UNTIL THE OTHER PERSON IS RECEP-
TIVE. When the other person makes a flat assertion, that is, a
definite, categorical statement, in opposition to your position, it
is pointless to try to move him off his position through the use
of information and logical argument. He is unreceptive and
simply will not absorb what you say.

If your arguments are very powerful so that it seems that any
reasonable person would have to succumb under their weight, it
will be difficult to resist the temptation to thrust them forward.
You say to yourself, "How can I miss? As soon as he hears what
I have to say, he will give way." This seductive illusion tempts
one into some very exasperating experiences and accounts for
a good many communication breakdowns.

Behind the thick walls of his psychological defenses he
scarcely hears your arguments. And those he does hear he
minimizes. You have to enter the domain of *his* thinking at this
point rather than trying to bring him into yours. He simply
doesn't want to move at all. So you have to come to him.

4. EXPLORE THE OTHER PERSON'S POSITION FOR WEAKNESS. You
have to lead him on an objective survey of his position until
you either find it sound, or you find a weakness. If you find it
sound, you cannot persuade him since his position is as good
as or better than yours. If you find a weakness, this weakness
then serves as an opening. When this weakness is encountered
his receptivity will go up. He will indicate this by some expression of self-doubt that perhaps there is something more that he
can do, or by some question about how he can strengthen this
weakness. This is the time for you to present your arguments.

Let's take some examples now to demonstrate the developing

of receptivity. In the case below a nurse is trying to persuade a patient.

The nurse says, "It would be a a good idea Mr. Jones for you to take a little walk up and down the ward. The doctor prescribed it."

The patient replies, "I'm tired. I don't feel like walking. Let me alone."

At this point the nurse might be tempted to marshall all the arguments for taking the walk, and present these to the patient. But the patient is obviously unreceptive. There is no doubt or questioning in his reply. His assertion is quite definite. Rather than attempting to storm his defenses with all the weight of her authority and logic it would be much better for her to try to inculcate some receptivity as follows.

The nurse says, "You sound a little upset."

"You'd be too if you were kept awake all night."

"Kept awake?"

"This character in the next bed snores and mumbles loud enough to wake an army."

"That can be hard to take. Especially when you need your sleep. But why take it out on yourself?"

Here, the nurse by offering sympathy, encourages the patient to move emotionally toward her. Then she tries to arouse a feeling of wanting to know more.

The patient asks, "What do you mean?" His receptivity is now higher as indicated by his asking a question.

The nurse replies, "Well, a little walk will be good for your circulation. It'll help you sleep better, too. If you have to put up with some irritations you might as well do what's good for you, also."

"Well, maybe you're right. Nobody else is going to do it for me. But I hope I get some sleep tonight."

When you're trying to persuade someone to abandon his own position and adopt yours it is better to first ask him to substantiate his position rather than to immediately give him your logic. If you know that your position is sounder than his, when ou ask him to substantiate his position, weaknesses will appear. T 1ese weaknesses will provide points of receptivity on his part. You can then penetrate with the logic of your position.

.'ou have to be alert here to counteract your own impulses. For when you want to persuade you are eager to get your arguments out. You have the feeling that since your position is sounder, as soon as you show him your arguments he will capitulate. The flaw in this is your assumption of his receptivity. You can't assume this. You must provide for it.

To illustrate this: suppose a manager wants to persuade a subordinate to change his way of handling a particular task. The manager suggests a new way but the subordinate claims that his own way is better. Many managers at this point will be tempted to advance arguments for the change. But this is not really as effective as asking the subordinate to tell why he thinks his way is better than the manager's.

The subordinate simply will not be receptive to the manager's arguments at this point and won't really be evaluating them objectively. He will be concentrating on developing arguments for his own position. Assuming in this case that the manager is right, the subordinate will be clinging to his position on an emotional basis and justifying it with wishful reasoning. As long as this reasoning is in a half-formed state inside him, and not put into words, it isn't subjected to logical scrutiny. But when he is drawn out and has to bring his ideas into the open where both he and the manager can examine it, its weaknesses will become apparent. At this point the subordinate will become uncertain of his position and this uncertainty brings with it receptivity.

Similarly, in a sales interview suppose the prospect says that he doesn't want to buy the salesman's higher-priced product because the lower-priced product (that the buyer is getting from another supplier) is doing a good job. The salesman might be tempted at this point to advance all the benefits of his higher-priced product. He may feel that these benefits will change the prospect's mind. But the prospect is not receptive, as indicated by his positive assertion that what he has now is working well.

Rather than telling about the benefits of his product at this point, it would be better for the salesman to explore the buyer's case that his present product is good enough. The salesman might ask the prospect to tell him about the product he is now using. For example, the salesman might inquire about how well the product lasts. How much trouble has it given? What kind of service has he been getting? How good is delivery? Other questions could be asked that might provide information for a favorable comparison of products.

As soon as a weakness occurs the salesman has an opening. Such a weakness can be quantified to dollars and cents, and this can be added to the cost of the competitive product. The new cost can then be compared with the price of the salesman's product. When the price of the competitive product plus its weaknesses exceeds the price of the salesman's product the salesman's case is made. And the prospect has participated in building the salesman's case. He therefore will be receptive to the conclusion.

Giving Unsolicited Advice

While you may wonder why advice-giving is included in a chapter on persuading, close examination reveals that they often have very much in common. Actually, unsolicited advising is essentially selling the other person on doing something you want him to do. People who shun the notion of trying to influence others or interfere in their actions will often rationalize their attempts to influence as merely giving advice, trying to be helpful. This self-deception is similar to that which occurs when one pours out his anger in what he calls "honest criticism," although this criticism is not asked for.

If a person's advice were not sought, why would he give it unless he were trying to influence? He wouldn't, of course, but he doesn't like to face the fact that he is trying to influence. Not facing this fact often leads to a failure in persuading since the individual holds back on using persuasive techniques and hopes that somehow the logic of his advice will prevail.

The first thing to do then when giving unsolicited advice is to face the fact that you are trying to persuade. And since you're trying to persuade you will need a state of receptivity in the other person.

You have to first draw him out and explore his position until he expresses some uncertainty or indicates that he wants your opinion. Then you can give your "advice." And since you are trying to sell him you must also give him inducements, benefits that will result from his following your advice.

If you don't wait for signs of receptivity and don't provide ways in which he will gain from following your suggestions, your advice-giving stands out nakedly as an attempt to control him. You are in effect making demands. This introduces into the interplay two other forces: his desire to please you, and his wish to exercise his independence. These forces may very well determine his response so that his reaction will be governed not by the sensibleness of your ideas, but by his emotional reactions to others' making demands.

These emotional forces—the wish to please versus the desire to exercise independence—can lead an individual to comply with or to oppose suggestions without sensibly evaluating them. His action is therefore not necessarily any commentary on the merit of the ideas since these emotional forces can move him to act against his own best interests.

If his eagerness to please extends to the point of being unable to say no, he is bound to do something sooner or later that is bad for himself. And if his need to assert independence is sufficiently strong, he is likely to grow touchy about suggestions given him. He may be too concerned with proving that he is capable of making his own decisions, and may be harassed by the feeling that anything he does that coincides with another person's suggestion represents a dependency on the other person.

He may forget entirely that it still remains his decision, to either accept or reject a suggestion.

The more a person's behavior is governed by his need to prove something about himself—whether it be that he is a good natured, cooperative individual by never saying no, or that he is an independent, self-directing person, by never saying yes—the less likely is he to be receptive to another person's logic. In such cases the ideas must be made to come from the person they're addressed to.

When you are trying to persuade an individual who is trying to prove what he is like, you have to give an impression of neutrality, almost of indifference to which course of action he takes. You should lay out the facts before him and ask him what he thinks. And if his position is contrary to the one you'd like him to adopt, rather than stating your case at this point it would be better to merely supply additional information and ask him to re-evaluate the situation. But maintain your neutral stand.

Even though the person who can't say no does what you suggest, it is unwise to exploit this weakness. Such an individual generally is annoyed with this weakness and is likely to let out his resentment at the person trying to influence him. It is better to encourage such a person to draw his own conclusions.

Giving advice when it is solicited is so different a process from giving unsolicited advice that they ought hardly to be called by the same name. The second isn't really giving advice at all but an attempt to persuade, to sell something. And it is subject to the same forces that apply in any sale.

Giving Reassurance

The giving of reassurance is essentially a form of persuading. For reassuring is an attempt to bring about a desired change in another person's feeling; and the attempt to change another person's reaction of any kind—whether thought or feeling—is persuasion.

Generally, reassurance is given to allay feelings of anxiety or depression. One may be worried over a difficult decision or the consequences of a particular course of action, or an impending event, or the impression one is making. Here reassurance is given to remove anxiety. Similarly, one may berate one's self for being stupid or selfish or ugly or lacking in some other way. And here reassurance is given to alleviate depressive feelings.

Since the giving of reassurance is an attempt at persuasion, as in other forms of persuasion, receptivity must first be established. Reassurance given immediately upon hearing another person express his worry or depression is less than helpful. Without the other person's receptivity, reassuring him can virtually increase his discomfort. Let's see how.

When a person is anxious or depressed he wants to talk about it. Giving him immediate reassurance implies that his feelings aren't worth talking about. If the problems can be answered so simply, why discuss them? This blocks his expression of feeling and keeps his emotions uncomfortably pent up. The resulting discomfort is likely to irritate him and he may feel this irritation toward the person giving him the immediate reassurance.

If you reassure a worried person with a glib, "Don't worry," or tell him immediately that he's not stupid or selfish or whatever he accuses himself of, he is made to feel wrong in some way for harboring these feelings. And he may also feel that you are not receptive to his talking out his feelings.

Before reassurance is given one should draw out the other person. Ask him to tell you a little more about it. When he has had a chance to talk out his feelings, thereby attaining a greater degree of comfort, you can then give him reassurance He is now more receptive to it.

Let him know that you are interested in hearing about his problem, about why he feels the way he does. As he talks out he is likely to attain greater perspective on it. It isn't likely to be so bad once he puts it into words. When it is inside him he is too close to it. When he gets it out in front of him you can help him look at it from different angles.

Then your reassurance takes on more meaning. It is tied

more specifically to what he has said. It guides him to a new vision of his problem.

Key Points In Persuading

A common reason why attempts to persuade fail is the view of persuasion as a forceful bending to one's will. This conception leads to forceful measures, the exertion of strength through powerful argument, an emphatic voice, and a manner that brooks no opposition.

These methods do not work simply because ideas are not absorbed by being pounded in from the outside. They are grasped by being reached for from within. The trick is to get the other person to reach for them. And he first has to be receptive to absorbing ideas before he will reach.

This willingness to reach is indicated by an expression of wanting to know something. This might take the form of a question or an expression of doubt or uncertainty. You have to wait therefore with your implanting of ideas until you observe these signs of reaching.

How do you bring a person to reach? Simply by drawing him out. When he feels positive or definite about something, he is not receptive. Your best move at this point is to get him to talk about his position. When he exhibits his position, holes are likely to appear at points where he hasn't thoroughly worked it out. At these points he is likely to express doubt or uncertainty or a desire for information.

Now he is receptive. Now he is reaching for what you can give him. Now is the time for you to present your ideas. He is ready to absorb them.

And once the ideas are presented feedback must be elicited to make the other person think; ideas have to be quantified; and in order to motivate him, benefits have to be given for adopting your point of view.

Emotions interfere with receptivity. They press for a giving out rather than a taking in. Therefore emotions must be discharged before ideas can be implanted.

This clearing away of emotions must be attended to first not only when information is to be offered but even when advice and reassurance are to be given for the emotion. If the person is in a heightened emotional state, one must resist the temptation to immediately feed in reassurance. It simply doesn't work and is only likely to intensify the emotion.

One must first draw out until the other person is relatively calm. Then advice or reassurance can be applied. The other person has discharged his feelings and is much closer to a receptive state. Now the person can be shown why the situation isn't as bad as it seems. And if the other person asks a question or expresses some uncertainty, he will be all the more receptive to the suggestions or reassurance given.

These techniques require practice and patience while one goes through the awkward, struggling stage in acquiring facility in using them. And one must resist all habits that push toward doing the opposite. Getting through to the mind of another person is often a painstaking effort. But your making this effort with others can bring with it the pleasure and productivity of achieving a meeting of minds and mutual good feeling. While without it there is only "sound and fury."

INDEX

Problems, field, 158, 159
Purpose, 19, 20, 45
  orientation of questions toward, 119

Q

Quantifying, 150-52
Questions, 6
  easy, 37-38
  high-structured, 42
  indicator of receptivity, 194
  insight, 111
  low-structured, 43-46
  meeting of minds and, 114, 119
  probing of audience, 186
  purposeful, 116-19
  stimulant to thought, 111, 112
  structuring of, 39-46
  yes-or-no, 43
Questioner, deceptive role of, 120
Questioning, 20, 21; see also Cross-examination, Information
  encouragement of group, 183-85, 186
  habit of, 163
  receptivity and, 194
  technique of, 37-46

R

Rage, 72; see also Anger
Rationalization, 99, 132
Reaction, emotional, 147
  discounting for, 151
  focusing, 126
  unpredictability of, 48, 49
Reactions, 112, 113
  implanting new, 189, 190
  securing of, 100, 122; see also Feedback
Readiness, factors in, 191
Reality, 59; see also Communication
  categorizing, 153
  coping with, 59
  language as description of, 145
  rejecting, 155
  separation of feelings from, 163
  words, 145, 146

Reason, 52, 53; see also Argument, Emotion, Logic
Reassurance, 17, 69, 70, 167, 198-200
  acceptance of anxiety, 138
  desire for, 16
  favorable comparison and, 71, 72
  method of, 137, 138
Receptivity, 192; see also Questions
  clues to, 201
  development of, 194-95
  establishment of, 191
  reassurance, 199
  signs of, 192, 200
Rejection, 12, 19, 165
Relationship, human, 165
  listening in, 172, 178
  role of giving, 166-68
  weakening of, 166
Relaxation, 37, 38
Relevance, 25, 96-98
  in conference, 187
  intrusions of emotion, 98
  logical, 25, 26
  loss of in group discussion, 180
  orders of, 31
  personality needs and, 95-99
  reliability of, 28, 29
Repetition, 5, 65, 102
  effective methods of, 43, 104, 105, 188
Reports, inadequate, 112, 113
Research, 111, 155
Resentment, 58, 148, 149
Resistance, 23, 37, 114
  assent as, 125
  cost, 44
  dealing with, 124-44
  evaluation of, 130-33
  handling of silent, 140
  implicit demand and, 77
  inventory as reason for, 141-42
  irrational, 129-31
  overcoming of sales, 93-94
  uncooperativeness, 139
Responses, 36, 189, 190; see also Persuading
Responsiveness, 175
Reticence, 20
Role, paternal, 85